Monetary, Fiscal and Trade Policies Series

AF681995

MEASURING THE ECONOMY: GDP AND NIPAs

Monetary, Fiscal and Trade Policies Series

Trade Policy in A Globalizing World
Yuki Watanabe and Haruto Yamashita
2009 ISBN: 978-1-60456-830-1

U.S. Trade with Developing Countries: Policy, Programs and Trends
Kalan R. Geisler
2009 ISBN: 978-1-60741-122-2

Measuring the Economy: GDP and NIPAs
Kemal Sahin
2009 ISBN: 978-1-60741-199-4

Taxation, Tax Policies and Income Taxes
Warren J. Berube and Camron N. Pinto
2009 ISBN: 978-1-60741-626-5

Challenges of the Post-Communist Financial-Currency Policy
Avtandil Silagadse and Micheil Tokmazishvili
2009. ISBN: 978-1-60741-150-5

Measuring the Economy: GDP and NIPAs
Kemal Sahin (Editor)
2009. ISBN: 978-1-60741-199-4

Monetary, Fiscal and Trade Policies Series

MEASURING THE ECONOMY: GDP AND NIPAS

KEMAL SAHIN
EDITOR

Nova Science Publishers, Inc.
New York

Copyright © 2009 by Nova Science Publishers, Inc.

All rights reserved. No part of this book may be reproduced, stored in a retrieval system or transmitted in any form or by any means: electronic, electrostatic, magnetic, tape, mechanical photocopying, recording or otherwise without the written permission of the Publisher.

For permission to use material from this book please contact us:
Telephone 631-231-7269; Fax 631-231-8175
Web Site: http://www.novapublishers.com

NOTICE TO THE READER

The Publisher has taken reasonable care in the preparation of this book, but makes no expressed or implied warranty of any kind and assumes no responsibility for any errors or omissions. No liability is assumed for incidental or consequential damages in connection with or arising out of information contained in this book. The Publisher shall not be liable for any special, consequential, or exemplary damages resulting, in whole or in part, from the readers' use of, or reliance upon, this material.

Independent verification should be sought for any data, advice or recommendations contained in this book. In addition, no responsibility is assumed by the publisher for any injury and/or damage to persons or property arising from any methods, products, instructions, ideas or otherwise contained in this publication.

This publication is designed to provide accurate and authoritative information with regard to the subject matter covered herein. It is sold with the clear understanding that the Publisher is not engaged in rendering legal or any other professional services. If legal or any other expert assistance is required, the services of a competent person should be sought. FROM A DECLARATION OF PARTICIPANTS JOINTLY ADOPTED BY A COMMITTEE OF THE AMERICAN BAR ASSOCIATION AND A COMMITTEE OF PUBLISHERS.

LIBRARY OF CONGRESS CATALOGING-IN-PUBLICATION DATA
Available upon request
ISBN: 978-1-60741-199-4

Published by Nova Science Publishers, Inc. ✣ New York

CONTENTS

Preface		**vii**
Chapter 1	Measuring the Economy: A Primer on GDP and the National Income and Product Accounts *Carlos M. Gutierrez, Cynthia A. Glassman, J. Steven Landefeld and Rosemary D. Marcuss*	**1**
Chapter 2	Methodology Papers: U.S. National Income and Product Accounts *Carlos M. Gutierrez, Cynthia A. Glassman, J. Steven Landefeld and Rosemary D. Marcuss*	**33**
Chapter 3	A Guide to the National Income and Product Accounts of the United States	**87**
Chapter 4	The Treatment of Federal Receipts and Expenditures in the National Income and Product Accounts *Congressional Budget Office*	**145**
Index		**167**

PREFACE

How fast is the economy growing? Is it speeding up or slowing down? How does the trade deficit affect economic growth? What's happening to the pattern of spending on goods and services in the economy? To answer these types of questions about the economy, economists and policymakers turn to the national income and product accounts (NIPAs) produced by the Bureau of Economic Analysis (BEA). Included in the NIPAs is gross domestic product (GDP), which measures the value of the goods and services produced by the U.S. economy in a given time period. This book is intended as an introduction to the GDP and NIPAs for the new user. It considers the transactions that occur in a simple economy in order to introduce such economic concepts that underlie the NIPA's. It describes the NIPA sectors for which economic activity is measured and the use of T-accounts to illustrate economic flows. An overview of the derivation of the NIPA measures are also given, including inflation-adjusted, or "real" estimates. In addition, references, organized by subject area are provided, for users interested in moving beyond an introduction to a more in-depth or advanced information about economic accounting and the NIPAs.

Chapter 1- This paper introduces new users to the basics of the U.S. national income and product accounts (NIPAs). It discusses the economic concepts that underlie the NIPAs, and it describes the seven NIPA summary accounts. The Primer also provides a brief overview of the derivation of the NIPA measures and a list of references for further information.

Chapter 2 - This paper provides a comprehensive explanation of the conceptual basis and framework of the U.S. national income and product accounts (NIPAs). It describes the structure and purpose of the U.S. economic accounts, discusses the relationship between business and financial accounting and national economic accounting, and presents a derivation of the seven NIPA summary accounts from generalized production, income and outlay, and capital accounts for each sector of the economy.

Chapter 3 - This guide presents information on the structure, definitions, and presentation that underlie the national income and product accounts (NIPAs) produced by the Bureau of Economic Analysis. The NIPAs show the composition of production and the distribution of incomes earned in production. Thus, they represent a critical element of the U.S. economic accounts, which are designed to provide a consistent and comprehensive picture of the Nation's economy. The NIPAs feature several widely followed measures of aggregate U.S. economic activity, including gross domestic product (GDP), gross domestic income (GDI), personal income, and personal saving among others.

Chapter 4 - This article describes how the treatment of federal receipts and expenditures in the national income and product accounts differs from the recording of federal revenues and outlays in the federal budget, as prepared by the Office of Management and Budget. It is one of a series of reports that the Congressional Budget Office (CBO) issues each year to fulfill section 202(e) of the Congressional Budget Act of 1974, which requires CBO to submit to the Committees on the Budget periodic reports about fiscal policy and to provide baseline projections of the federal budget. Most recently, in response to that requirement, CBO issued *The Budget and Economic Outlook: An Update* (August 2008).

In: Measuring the Economy: GDP and NIPAs ISBN: 978-1-60741-199-4
Editor: Kemal Sahin © 2009 Nova Science Publishers, Inc.

Chapter 1

MEASURING THE ECONOMY: A PRIMER ON GDP AND THE NATIONAL INCOME AND PRODUCT ACCOUNTS*

Carlos M. Gutierrez, Cynthia A. Glassman, J. Steven Landefeld and Rosemary D. Marcuss

ACKNOWLEDGMENTS

Stephanie H. McCulla and Shelly Smith of the National Income and Wealth Division, Bureau of Economic Analysis (BEA), U.S. Department of Commerce, prepared this Primer.

Brent R. Moulton, Associate Director for National Economic Accounts at BEA, and Carol E. Moylan, Chief of the National Income and Wealth Division at BEA, provided overall guidance.

PREFACE

This paper introduces new users to the basics of the U.S. national income and product accounts (NIPAs). It discusses the economic concepts that underlie the

* This is an edited, excerpted and augmented edition of a Bureau of Economic Analysis, U.S. Department of Commerce publication.

NIPAs, and it describes the seven NIPA summary accounts. The Primer also provides a brief overview of the derivation of the NIPA measures and a list of references for further information.

Comments and questions about the NIPA Primer are invited. Please contact BEA's National Income and Wealth Division, 1441 L St. NW, BE–54, Washington, DC 20230 or by e-mail at <GDPniwd@BEA.gov>.

How fast is the economy growing? Is it speeding up or slowing down? How does the trade deficit affect economic growth? What's happening to the pattern of spending on goods and services in the economy?

To answer these types of questions about the economy, economists and policymakers turn to the national income and product accounts (NIPAs) produced by the Bureau of Economic Analysis (BEA). The NIPAs are a set of economic accounts that provide information on the value and composition of output produced in the United States during a given period and on the distribution and uses of the income generated by that production. Featured in the NIPAs is gross domestic product (GDP), which measures the value of the goods and services produced by the U.S. economy in a given time period.

GDP is one of the most comprehensive and closely watched economic statistics: It is used by the White House and Congress to prepare the Federal budget, by the Federal Reserve to formulate monetary policy, by Wall Street as an indicator of economic activity, and by the business community to prepare forecasts of economic performance that provide the basis for production, investment, and employment planning.

But to fully understand an economy's performance, one must ask not only "What is GDP?" (or "What is the value of the economy's output?"), but other questions such as: "How much of the increase in GDP is the result of inflation and how much is an increase in real output?" "Who is producing the output of the economy?" "What output are they producing?" "What income is generated as a result of that production?" and "How is that income used (to consume more output, to invest, or to save for future consumption or investment)?"

Thus, while GDP is the featured measure of the economy's output, it is only *one summary measure*. The answers to the follow-up questions are found by looking at other measures found in the NIPAs; these include personal income, corporate profits, and government spending. Because the economy is so complex, the NIPAs simplify the information by organizing it in a way that illustrates the processes taking place.

This paper is intended as an introduction to the NIPAs for the new user. It begins by considering the transactions that occur in a simple economy in order to introduce the economic concepts that underlie the NIPAs. Next, it describes the

NIPA sectors for which economic activity is measured and the use of T-accounts to illustrate economic flows. The third section introduces the seven summary accounts of the NIPAs and includes descriptions of the significant aggregates that they contain. The fourth section provides an overview of the derivation of the NIPA measures, including inflation-adjusted, or "real," estimates. The last section provides references, organized by subject area, for users interested in moving beyond an introduction to more in-depth or advanced information about economic accounting and the NIPAs.

Conceptual Basis of the Accounts

The Circular Flow of Income and Expenditures

To better understand the economy and the NIPAs, consider a simple economy consisting solely of businesses and individuals, as reflected in the circular flow diagram below:

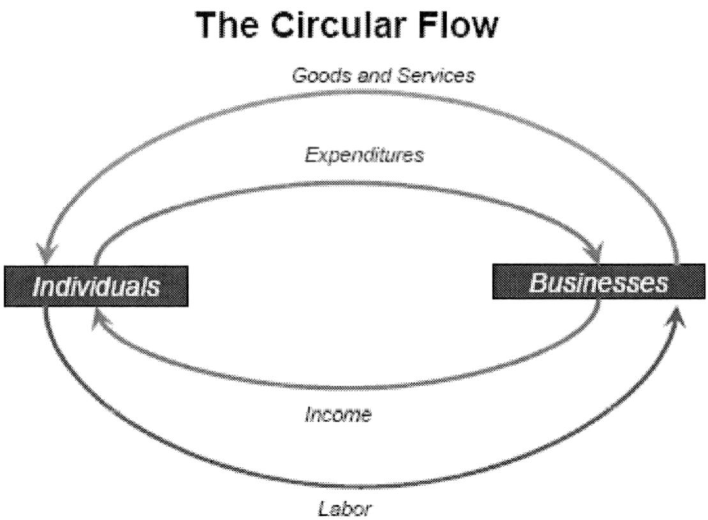

In this simple economy, individuals provide the labor that enables businesses to produce goods and services. These activities are represented by the green lines in the diagram above.

Alternatively, one can think of these transactions in terms of the monetary flows that occur. Businesses provide individuals with income (in the form of compensation) in exchange for their labor. That income is, in turn, spent on the goods and services businesses produce. These activities are represented by the blue lines in the diagram above.

Economic Concepts in the NIPAs

The circular flow diagram illustrates the interdependence of the "flows," or activities, that occur in the economy, such as the production of goods and services (or the "output" of the economy) and the income generated from that production. The circular flow also illustrates the equality between the income earned from production and the value of goods and services produced.

Of course, the total economy is much more complicated than the illustration above. An economy involves interaction between not only individuals and businesses, but also Federal, state, and local governments and residents of the rest of the world. Not shown in this simple illustration of the economy are the other resources used in the production of output such as investment in physical capital (fixed assets such as equipment, structures, and software), flows of financial capital (such as stocks, bonds, and bank deposits), and the contributions of these flows to the accumulation of fixed assets.

The NIPAs provide a framework for presenting actual measures of these economic flows.

Output

The featured measure of output in the NIPAs is GDP. GDP measures the value of final goods and services produced in the United States in a given period of time. While GDP is used as an indicator of economic progress, it is not a measure of well-being (for example, it does not account for rates of poverty, crime, or literacy).

The following are several points to keep in mind when considering the output of the economy.

1. GDP Includes Market Production and Some Non- Market Production

GDP is composed of goods and services that are produced for sale in the "market"—the generic term referring to the forum for economic transactions—and of nonmarket goods and services—those that are not sold in the market, such as the defense services provided by the Federal Government, the education services provided by local governments, the emergency housing or health care services provided by nonprofit institutions serving households (such as the Red Cross), and the housing services provided by and for persons who own and live in their home (referred to as "owner-occupants"). However, not all productive activity is included in GDP. Some activities, such as the care of one's own children, unpaid volunteer work for charities, or illegal or black-market activities, are not included because they are difficult to accurately measure and value.

2. Whenever Possible, GDP Is Valued at Market Prices

The NIPAs value market goods and services using prices set by the market. This approach provides a common unit of measurement (dollars) that facilitates comparisons of the various goods and services that make up economic activity. Using market values also facilitates the analysis of the impacts on the economy of events such as the implementation of government programs or the occurrence of natural disasters.

In some cases, market prices do not fully reflect the value of a good or service, and may include some types of services where an actual exchange has not occurred. In these cases, the value of the good or service produced is "imputed" from similar market transactions. Imputations measure the value of goods and services that are not fully reflected in market prices. Examples of imputed measures in the NIPAs include the value of compensation-in-kind (such as meals provided by employers) and the value of owner-occupied housing. For more information on owner-occupied housing, see the box on page 5, "An Imputation for the Services of Owner-Occupied Housing."

In cases where there are no similar market transactions available to impute a value of the goods or service being produced, the output of these services is valued by estimating the input costs (such as employee compensation and purchases of materials and supplies) of providing the services.

3. GDP Is a Measure of Current Production, Not Sales

In the NIPAs, output measures when a good or service is produced, not when that good or service is sold. For example, an automaker may produce a car in one period and sell it in a later period. In the first period, the production of the car is recorded in GDP as an addition to inventories, a component of investment. In the later period, the sale of the car is recorded as a consumer expenditure and is offset by the withdrawal of the car from inventories.

4. GDP Includes the Value of "Final" Goods and Services Only

In the measurement of GDP, *final* products are those that are consumed and not used in a later stage of production, those that are sold to foreign residents, those that are durable goods and structures used to produce other goods and last more than a year, and those that may be inventoried for future consumption. When considering the production process for the entire economy, intermediate products—that is, goods and services that are used as inputs in the production process (and will not contribute to future production)—are excluded, so that the measure of output is an unduplicated total.

For example, consider a simple economy with one product, bread, which is produced in three stages:

1 Wheat is grown, harvested, and sold for $1 by a farmer (for simplification, it is assumed the wheat is produced using no intermediate products);
2 The wheat is used by a miller to produce flour, which is sold for $3; and
3 The flour is used by a baker to produce bread, which is sold to a consumer for $7.

This information is summarized in exhibit 1:

Exhibit 1.

	Intermediate product	Income	Sales
Farmer, wheat	$0	$1	$1
Miller, flour	$1	$2	$3
Baker, bread	$3	$4	$7
Total	$4	$7	$11

When the miller purchases $1 worth of wheat from the farmer to produce flour and then sells the flour to the baker for $3, the $3 the miller charges for the flour includes the $1 price of the wheat (an intermediate product) plus the $2 value added by his own resources (in this example, his labor). When the baker makes the flour into bread and sells the bread to a consumer for $7, the $7 the baker charges includes the $3 value of the flour (an intermediate product) and the $4 value added by his own resources. The value of the final product—the bread—is the price paid by the consumer ($7); the bread is recognized as the final product because it is eaten by the consumer and not used in another production process. If the total sales of the wheat, the flour, and the bread were all included, the aggregate value ($1 + $3 + $7, or $11) would overstate the value of production by triple-counting the value of the wheat and double-counting the value of the flour.

5. GDP Can Be Measured in Three Different Ways

The nature of economic activity reflected in the circular flow diagram suggests two ways to measure GDP. First, GDP can be measured as the sum of expenditures, or purchases, by final users. This is known as the *expenditures approach* (and is illustrated by the formula familiar to students of economics:

GDP = Consumption + Investment + Government spending + eXports – iMports)

and is used to identify the final goods and services purchased by persons, businesses, governments, and foreigners. Second, because the market price of a final good or service will reflect all of the incomes earned and costs incurred in production, GDP can also be measured as the sum of these charges. This is known as the *income approach* and is used to examine the purchasing power of households and the financial status of business income.

In addition, GDP can also be measured either as total sales less the value of intermediate inputs or as the sum of the "value added" at each stage of the production process. The *value-added approach* to measuring GDP is central to the U.S. industry accounts and is used to analyze the industrial composition of U.S. outputs.

These three approaches can be illustrated using the information from exhibit 1.

- As demonstrated in point 4 below, GDP can be derived as the sum of final expenditures for bread, which is the $7 spent by consumers.
- It can be derived as the sum of the incomes earned in the production of bread—that is, as the sum of the $1 earned by the farmer for his labor, the $2 earned by the miller for his labor, and the $4 earned by the baker for his labor.
- It can be derived as the value added, or total output less intermediate products, across all industries—that is, the $1 of output by the farmer, plus the $3 of output by the miller, plus the $7 of output by the baker minus the $0 of intermediate inputs by the farmer, minus the $1 of intermediate inputs by the miller, minus the $3 of intermediate inputs by the baker ($11 – $4 = $7).

	Intermediate product	Income = value added	Sales = output
Farmer, wheat	$0	$1	$1
Miller, flour	$1	$2	$3
Baker, bread	$3	$4	$7
Total	$4	$7	$11

Output (sum of final expenditures) = Total income earned from production.
Value added = Total output – Total intermediate products.

6. GDP Captures Output Produced in the United States

GDP is a measure of the goods and services produced by labor and property located *within the United States* (in the NIPAs, the United States comprises the 50 states and the District of Columbia). Thus, GDP includes the output of U.S. offices or establishments of foreign companies located in the United States, and it excludes the output of foreign offices or establishments of U.S. companies located outside the United States. This treatment aligns GDP with other key U.S. statistics associated with the domestic economy, such as population and employment.

7. GDP Is a "Gross" Measure

GDP reflects production in a given time period, regardless of whether that production is used for immediate consumption, for investment in new fixed assets or inventories, or for replacing depreciated fixed assets. Economic depreciation, or the consumption of fixed capital (CFC), is a measure of the amount that would need to be "set aside" to cover the aging, wear and tear, accidental damage, and obsolescence of existing fixed assets. Subtracting CFC from GDP leaves "net domestic product," which is a measure of current production that excludes the investment that is necessary to replace fixed assets as they wear out. Thus, net domestic product is a measure that indicates how much of the Nation's output is available for consumption or for adding to the Nation's wealth.

Income

In addition to GDP, which is measured using the final expenditures approach, the NIPAs also present gross domestic income (GDI), which is GDP measured using the income approach. As noted above, this approach measures output as the sum of the incomes accruing to the owners of the factors of production (capital and labor) and to governments. In other words, as the circular flow diagram suggests, income is equal to product (GDI is equal to GDP).

The NIPAs also include other measures of income. Two of these are gross national income (GNI) and personal income. GNI, the most comprehensive measure of a nation's income, is calculated as GDI plus income receipts from the rest of the world less income payments to the rest of the world. As such, it is a measure of income from production that accrues to U.S. residents, regardless of where that productive activity is located. Its companion production measure is gross national product (GNP). Personal income is the income received by persons from participation in production (including compensation and interest and dividend income) and from transfers from government and businesses. Personal income is closely monitored both as an indicator of economic activity and as a predictor of future spending.

It is important to note that the income measures in the NIPAs do not count gains or losses resulting from changes in the prices of assets (that is, capital gains or losses) as income, because a gain for one represents a loss for another.

An Imputation for the Services of Owner-Occupied Housing

Within GDP, personal consumption expenditures include the consumption of housing services by persons who own the housing that they occupy (referred to as "owner-occupants") as well as by those who rent their housing. The imputation ensures that GDP will not change if a house is rented by a landlord or lived in by its owner.

When a landlord provides housing services to a tenant in exchange for payment—rent—the transaction appears on the product side of the accounts as personal con sumption expenditures for housing services and on the income side as rental income of persons. If the NIPAs were strictly constrained to items traded on the market, the measurement would end there. That is, the housing services provided to owner-occupants would be excluded from GDP because homeownership involves no market exchange of housing services for rent. Under this treatment, GDP would increase if a home were rented to a tenant rather than occupied by the homeowner (and would decrease if a home were occupied by the home owner rather than rented to a tenant).

To prevent such a variance in GDP from occurring, the NIPAs treat home ownership as if the owner-occupants rent their homes to themselves. The value of these housing services is based on the rents charged for similar tenant-occupied housing. Therefore, GDP is based on the number and quality of housing units in service and will not change if a house switches from being rented by a landlord to being lived in by its owner. On the income side of the accounts, the owner-occupant is treated similarly to a business. Expenses associated with owner-occupied housing, such as depreciation, maintenance and repairs, property taxes, and mortgage interest, are deducted from the value of the housing services, leaving a profit-like remainder of income, "rental income of persons."

NIPA Sectors

From the NIPAs, one can determine who demands the goods and services that are produced, or one can examine who supplies the output being produced. Three major types of producers (or sectors) are recognized:

Businesses. This sector engages in the production and sale of goods and services for profit, or at least for a price that approximates the costs of production. The sector comprises all for-profit corporate and noncorporate private entities and certain other entities that are treated as businesses in the NIPAs, including mutual financial institutions, private noninsured pension funds, cooperatives, nonprofit organizations that primarily serve businesses, Federal Reserve banks, federally sponsored credit agencies, and government enterprises. Government enterprises are government agencies—such as the U.S. Postal Service or state government-run utilities—that cover a substantial portion of their operating costs by selling goods and services to the public.

Households and institutions. This sector engages in the production of household services—that is the housing services provided to homeowners, the goods and services provided by nonprofit institutions, and the compensation paid to domestic workers. The sector consists of private household workers, owner-occupants, and nonprofit institutions servings households (such as Goodwill Industries International).

General governments. This sector receives revenues from taxes and other sources and uses these revenues to provide public goods and services, such as education and defense, and transfer payments, such as social security or Medicaid benefits. The sector includes Federal, state, and local government agencies, except for government enterprises.

In addition, various measures are shown for subsets of these sectors (or subsectors). For example, separate measures are available for farm businesses, nonfarm businesses, corporations, noncorporate businesses, households, nonprofit institutions serving households, Federal Government, and state and local governments.

The T-account

AT-account offers another way to illustrate the flows of the economy. More detailed than the cir cular flow diagram, it is a two-sided table that matches "sources " of funds on the right, or credit side, with "uses " on the left, or debit side. The entries on each side sum to a total shown at the bottom; the totals on each side are equal. The example below presents a very simple "income and outlay" account for an individual.

The right side of the account shows an individual's sources of income: Compensation (primarily wages and salaries) and the interest and dividends received from the ownership of assets (such as bonds or stocks). The sum of these sources is "total income." The left side shows the individual's uses of income: Consumption (purchases of goods and services), tax payments, and saving. The sum of these uses is "total expenditures and saving." As with the circular flow, the T-account shows that income equals expenditures.

The structure of the T-account provides two analytical benefits. First, because it is an identity, it enables one to identify and estimate a “balancing item” between the two sides of the account: In the example, the difference between the individual’s total income on the right side and the individual’s consumption and tax payments on the left side provides a measure of the individual’s saving. Second, when constructed for more than one economic sector, the T-accounts provide a “double-entry” system in which a source of income in an account for one sector also appears as a use of income in the account of another sector. This accounting framework tracks the flow of economic activity from one sector to another.

Income and Outlay Account for an Individual

Uses of Income		Sources of Income	
Consumption	50	Compensation	70
Tax payments	20	Interest received	20
Saving	30	Dividends received	10
Total Expenditures and Saving	100	Total Income	100

THE SEVEN NIPA SUMMARY ACCOUNTS

In the NIPAs, the flows of production-related activities and income between sectors of the economy are summarized in the seven accounts presented below. The parenthetical numbers following each entry in an account indicate the table and line item location of the “counter-entries,” or the flow from one sector of the economy to another.

The first account, the Domestic Income and Product Account, displays the expenditure and income approaches to measuring GDP. The right-hand side of the account shows the expenditures on final output by consumers, private business, governments and foreigners. The left-hand side of the account shows the incomes that are generated in the production of that output.

Account 2 presents the sources and uses of income for private enterprises (that is, corporate and noncorporate businesses and households and institutions in their role as producers). Account 3 presents personal income and outlays (that is, the income and outlays of households and nonprofit institutions, except for the outlays they make as producers). Account 4 presents government receipts and expenditures. Account 5, the Foreign Transactions Current Account, summarizes the current transactions relating to production, income, and outlays of the United

States with the rest of the world. Accounts 6 and 7 are capital accounts; they reflect the transactions that contribute to the accumulation of fixed assets and inventories by showing the Nation's saving and the use of that saving for investment in fixed assets and inventories and for net lending or borrowing. Specifically, account 6 is a consolidated "saving-investment" account for the domestic sectors of the United States, and account 7 summarizes the capital transactions of the United States with the rest of the world.

Account 1. Domestic Income and Product Account

Account 1 is a production account for the United States: The right, or "product" side, of account 1 shows the total final output produced in the Nation organized by type of expenditure, and the left, or "income" side, shows the incomes and other costs incurred in production. The summary measure of production on the right side—GDP—is defined as the market value of final goods and services produced by labor and property within the United States during a given period.

The entries on the right side of account 1 show the approach used by BEA for deriving GDP: It is measured using the expenditures approach—that is, as the sum of purchases by final users. Specifically, GDP is the sum of:

- *Personal consumption expenditures* consist of purchases of goods and services by households and by nonprofit institutions serving households (NPISHs). These goods and services include imputed expenditures on items such as the services of housing by a homeowner (the equivalent of rent), financial and insurance services for which there is no explicit charge, and medical care provided to individuals and financed by government or by private insurance.
- *Gross private domestic investment* consists of purchases of fixed assets (equipment, software, and structures) by private businesses that contribute to production and have a useful life of more than one year, of purchases of homes by households, and of private business investment in inventories. Inventory investment, which is shown as "change in private inventories," includes the value of goods produced during a period but not sold, less sales of goods from inventories that were produced in previous periods. It is measured as ending period less beginning period inventories valued at current prices (and is equivalent to additions to, less withdrawals from, inventories), Intermediate inputs, which become an

integral part of the final product and do not contribute to future production, are not included in investment.

- *Exports* consists of goods and services that are sold or transferred by U.S. residents to residents of the rest of the world.
- *Imports,* which is deducted in the calculation of GDP, consists of goods and services that are sold or transferred by the rest of the world to U.S. residents. The value of imports is already included in the other expenditure components of GDP, because market transactions do not distinguish the source of the goods and services. Therefore, imports must be deducted in order to derive a measure of total *domestic* output. Deducting total imports purchased by all sectors from total exports, rather than deducting each sector's imports from its total expenditures, provides an analytically useful measure—net exports—that enables one to examine the effects of foreign trade on the economy.
- *Government consumption expenditures and gross investment* measures final expenditures by Federal, state, and local governments. "Government consumption expenditures" represents the value of goods and services provided to the public by governments (such as defense or education). "Gross investment" consists of government purchases of equipment, software, and structures to use in producing those goods and services. These expenditures do not include government spending for social benefit programs (such as Medicaid), interest payments, and subsidies.

The left—or income—side of the Domestic Income and Product Account measures output using the income approach, as the sum of all the incomes earned and costs incurred in production. Specifically, the left side shows GDI as the sum of the income earned by labor (compensation of employees), by governments (taxes on production and imports less subsidies), and by entrepreneurs (net operating surplus, which is a profits-like measure for private enterprises, described below, and for government enterprises), and the consumption of fixed capital. These entries appear again as sources of income in accounts 2 through 5.

In theory, GDI should be equal to GDP. In practice, differences in the source data used to estimate the two measures result in a "statistical discrepancy," which, in the NIPAs, is calculated as GDP less GDI. Because the source data used to develop the product-side estimates of the account are based on more comprehensive surveys and censuses, BEA considers them more reliable. Therefore, the statistical discrepancy appears as a component on the income side of the account.

Table A. Summary National Income and Product Accounts, 2006—Continues
[Billions of dollars]
Account 1. Domestic Income and Product Account

Line		
1	Compensation of employees, paid	7,454.8
2	Wage and salary accruals.	6,032.2
3	Disbursements (3–12 and 5–11).	6,024.7
4	Wage accruals less disbursements (4–9 and 6–11)	7.5
5	Supplements to wages and salaries (3–14)	1,422.6
6	Taxes on production and imports (4–16).	967.3
7	*Less:* Subsidies (4–8)	49.7
8	Net operating surplus.	3,225.3
9	Private enterprises (2–19)	3,239.2
10	Current surplus of government enterprises (4–26)	–13.9
11	Consumption of fixed capital (6–13)..	1,615.2
12	Gross domestic income	13,212.8
13	Statistical discrepancy (6–19).	–18.1
14	GROSS DOMESTIC PRODUCT	13,194.7
15	Personal consumption expenditures (3–3)	9,224.5
16	Durable goods	1,048.9
17	Nondurable goods	2,688.0
18	Services.	5,487.6
19	Gross private domestic investment.	2,209.2
20	Fixed investment (6–2)	2,162.5
21	Nonresidential .	1,397.7
22	Structures	405.1
23	Equipment and software..	992.6
24	Residential.	764.8
25	Change in private inventories (6–4).	46.7
26	Net exports of goods and services	–762.0
27	Exports (5–1)	1,467.6
28	Imports (5–9)	2,229.6
29	Government consumption expenditures and gross investment (4–1 and 6–3).	2,523.0
30	Federal	932.5
31	National defense.	624.3
32	Nondefense	308.2
33	State and local..	1,590.5
34	GROSS DOMESTIC PRODUCT	13,194.7

Account 2. Private Enterprise Income Account

Line		
1	Income payments on assets	3,109.3
2	Interest and miscellaneous payments (3–20 and 4–21)	2,946.8
3	Dividend payments to the rest of the world (5–14).	91.4
4	Reinvested earnings on foreign direct investment in the United States (5–15)	71.1
5	Business current transfer payments (net)	90.2
6	To persons (net) (3–24).	27.2
7	To government (net) (4–24)	60.6
8	To the rest of the world (net) (5–19)	2.5
9	Proprietors' income with inventory valuation and capital consumption	1,006.7
10	adjustments (3–17)	54.5
11	Rental income of persons with capital consumption adjustment (3–18)	1,553.7
12	Corporate profits with inventory valuation and capital consumption adjustments	453.9
13	Taxes on corporate income	435.5
14	To government (4–17)	18.4
15	To the rest of the world (5–19)	1,099.8
16	Profits after tax with inventory valuation and capital consumption adjustments	698.9
17	Net dividends (3–21 and 4–22)... consumption adjustments (6–10)	400.9
18	USES OF PRIVATE ENTERPRISE INCOME	5,814.5
19	Net operating surplus (1–9)...	3,239.2
Line		
20	Income receipts on assets..	2,575.3
21	Interest (3–20)	2,155.5
22	Dividend receipts from the rest of the world (5–6).	167.2
23	Reinvested earnings on U.S. direct investment abroad (5–7).	252.6
24	SOURCES OF PRIVATE ENTERPRISE INCOME.	5,814.5

Account 2. The Private Enterprise Income Account

The right side of account 2 shows the sources of private enterprise income, and the left side shows the distribution of this income among the various types of private enterprises, facilitating the subsequent presentation of related counter-entries on the sources side of the personal, government, and foreign accounts (accounts 3, 4, and 5, respectively). Private enterprises include most of the business sector and part of the household sector— specifically, the ownership of housing. Private enterprises do not include government enterprises, as they are not privately owned.

On the right side of account 2, sources of private enterprise income include both income from current production—net operating surplus—and income from the provision of financial capital—income receipts on assets. The net operating surplus reflects the incomes earned by all private enterprises from production after deducting operating costs (such as employee compensation and taxes on production and imports). Income receipts on assets reflects income that accrues to the providers of financial capital—holders of debt or stock. It comprises interest receipts, dividend receipts from the rest of the world, and businesses' share of the reinvested earnings of their foreign affiliates. (Because the account consolidates the earnings of all U.S. businesses, receipts and payments of dividends between domestic businesses cancel each other.)

The left side of the account shows the distribution of income among corporate enterprises (corporate profits), unincorporated enterprises owned by persons (proprietors' income), and homeowners (rental income of persons). It also shows summary information on the income distributed to the providers of financial capital (income payments on assets), not distinguished by sector in this account, and on the receipts of transfer payments.

Proprietors' income and rental income of persons reappear as sources of income on the right side of the personal income and outlay account, and net interest and dividend payments by enterprises equal the sum of net interest and dividends received by all other sectors. Only corporate profits (which is similar to net operating surplus but is measured after the deduction of interest payments) does not have a counter-entry on the sources side of a separate income and outlay account; a separate account for corporations is unnecessary because the detailed entries in account 2 show the use of this income for tax payments, dividend payments, and for undistributed corporate profits (which can be thought of as a measure of corporate saving).[1]

Corporate profits is one of the most closely followed measures of economic activity because it provides a summary measure of U.S. corporate financial health. Further, undistributed profits, a source of retained earnings, provide much of the funding for investment in structures and equipment that contributes to the Nation's productive capacity.

---

[1] Likewise, a separate account for the business sector as a whole—that is, private enterprises and government enterprises—is unnecessary because the sources and uses of government enterprise income are reflected in account 4.

Account 3. Personal Income and Outlay Account

Line		
1	Personal current taxes (4–15)	1,354.3
2	Personal outlays..	9,590.3
3	Personal consumption expenditures (1–15)	9,224.5
4	Personal interest payments (3–20)	238.0
5	Personal current transfer payments	127.8
6	To government (4–25)	78.9
7	To the rest of the world (net) (5–17)	48.9
8	Personal saving (6–9)	38.8
9	PERSONAL TAXES, OUTLAYS, AND SAVING.	10,983.4
10	Compensation of employees, received.	7,440.8
11	Wage and salary disbursements	6,018.2
12	Domestic (1–3 less 5–11)	6,015.3
13	Rest of the world (5–3)	2.9
14	Supplements to wages and salaries (1–5)	1,422.6
15	Employer contributions for employee pension and insurance funds..	970.7
16	Employer contributions for government social insurance	451.8
17	Proprietors' income with inventory valuation and capital consumption adjustments (2–9)..	1,006.7
18	Rental income of persons with capital consumption adjustment (2–10).	54.5
19	Personal income receipts on assets	1,796.5
20	Personal interest income (2–2 and 3–4 and 4–7 and 5–5 less 2–21 less 4–21 less 5–13)	1,100.2
21	Personal dividend income (2–16 less 4–22).	696.3
22	Personal current transfer receipts	1,612.5
23	Government social benefits (4–4)..	1,585.3
24	From business (net) (2–6)	27.2
25	*Less:* Contributions for government social insurance (4–19)	927.6
26	PERSONAL INCOME	10,983.4

Account 3. The Personal Income and Outlay Account

The personal income and outlay account shows the sources and uses of income of individuals, enterprises that are owned by households, and nonprofit institutions that serve households.

The right side of the account features the components of personal income, which is the current income received by persons from all sources; that is, from their contributions to production (from their labor or from owning a home or business), from transfers from government and businesses, and from the ownership of financial assets (such as interest and dividends).[2] The largest source of income for individuals is compensation, which they receive for their labor; compensation includes employee and employer contributions to retirement and pension plans. Proprietors' income is the income received by individuals for their labor and use of capital. Rental income is the income received by persons from their rental of property. Other components of personal income include interest income, dividend income, and current transfers. Current transfers include government social benefits payments for programs such as social security and Medicaid. Lastly, "contributions for government social insurance" (mandatory contributions to social insurance programs such as social security) is deducted in the measurement of personal income because the benefits accruing from these contributions are already reflected in current transfers.

The left side of the account shows that personal income is used primarily for consumption of goods and services. The entry for "personal consumption expenditures" flows directly into account 1, and is, in fact, the largest component of GDP. In other words, households are the largest consumers of U.S. final product. The other entries illustrate that households also pay taxes and make interest and transfer payments. The difference between a household's income and the sum of these outlays is its saving.

Account 4. The Government Receipts and Expenditures Account

This account is also an income and outlay account, showing—for Federal, state, and local governments (including government enterprises)—total receipts of income on the right side and the current uses of income (including saving) on the left side. The bulk of government income is derived from the receipt of taxes; governments also receive contributions for government social insurance, income receipts on assets, transfers (such as donations, fees, and fines), and the current surplus of government enterprises.

The left side of the account features the uses of government receipts, which include current expenditures and government saving. Government transfer payments, which account for a large share of government current expenditures, are payments for which no current good or service is provided by the recipient, such

[2] Personal income does not include holding gains or losses associated with changes in asset prices, as this type of change reflects a change in wealth rather than a change in productive activity.

as unemployment benefits. “Other current transfer payments to the rest of the world” consists of U.S. Government military and nonmilitary grants to foreign governments. Interest payments reflect interest paid on public debt, and subsidies refers to the provision of subsidies to businesses.

The balancing item of the account is net government saving, which shows the difference between current receipts and current expenditures. Because of differences in coverage and timing, Federal Government net saving in the NIPAs is not equal to the well- known measure of the Federal Government’s unified budget surplus or deficit, which is an administrative cash-flow measure derived from the Treasury Department’s Federal budget statements and which includes both current and capital receipts and expenditures. The NIPA measure of government saving represents the portion of current expenditures that are covered by current receipts rather than by other methods of financing.

Account 4. Government Receipts and Expenditures Account

Line		
1	Consumption expenditures (1–29) .	2,089.3
2	Current transfer payments...	1,618.3
3	Government social benefits.	1,588.7
4	To persons (3–23)	1,585.3
5	To the rest of the world (5–18) .	3.3
6	Other current transfer payments to the rest of the world (net) (5–18)	29.6
7	Interest payments (3–20)	372.9
8	Subsidies (1–7)	49.7
9	*Less:* Wage accruals less disbursements (1–4)..	0.0
10	Net government saving (6–12)	–195.4
11	Federal	–220.0
12	State and local	24.6
13	GOVERNMENT CURRENT EXPENDITURES AND NET SAVING.	3,934.8
14	Current tax receipts	2,769.8
15	Personal current taxes (3–1).	1,354.3
16	Taxes on production and imports (1–6)	967.3
17	Taxes on corporate income (2–13)	435.5
18	Taxes from the rest of the world (5–18)	12.6
19	Contributions for government social insurance (3–25)	927.6
20	Income receipts on assets	111.9
21	Interest and miscellaneous receipts (2–2 and 3–20)	109.3
22	Dividends (3–21)	2.6
23	Current transfer receipts	139.5
24	From business (net) (2–7).	60.6
25	From persons (3–6)	78.9
26	Current surplus of government enterprises (1–10)	–13.9
27	GOVERNMENT CURRENT RECEIPTS	3,934.8

Account 5. Foreign Transactions Current Account

Line		
1	Exports of goods and services (1–27)	1,467.6
2	Income receipts from the rest of the world	691.4
3	Wage and salary receipts (3–13)	2.9
4	Income receipts on assets .	688.6
5	Interest (3–20)	268.8
6	Dividends (2–22)	167.2
7	Reinvested earnings on U.S. direct investment abroad (2–23)	252.6
8	CURRENT RECEIPTS FROM THE REST OF THE WORLD.	2,159.0
9	Imports of goods and services (1–28)	2,229.6
10	Income payments to the rest of the world..	633.4
11	Wage and salary payments (1–3).	9.4
12	Income payments on assets .	624.0
13	Interest (3–20)	461.5
14	Dividends (2–3)	91.4
15	Reinvested earnings on foreign direct investment in the United States (2–4)	71.1
16	Current taxes and transfer payments to the rest of the world (net).	90.1
17	From persons (net) (3–7)..	48.9
18	From government (net) (4–5 and 4–6 less 4–18)	20.3
19	From business (net) (2–8 and 2–14).	20.9
20	Balance on current account, national income and product accounts (7–1)	–794.1
21	CURRENT PAYMENTS TO THE REST OF THE WORLD AND BALANCE ON CURRENT ACCOUNT	2,159.0

Account 5. Foreign Transactions Current Account

Account 5 summarizes all of the current transactions of the United States with the rest of the world. It is shown from the perspective of the rest of the world; that is, U.S. imports from other countries are shown as a source of income for the rest of the world on the right side of the account, and exports of U.S. goods are shown as a use of that income on the left side. Similarly, payments made to the rest of the world from the left side of accounts 2, 3, and 4 (compensation, interest, dividends, or transfers) are shown as sources of foreign income, while the corresponding receipts by residents of the United States are shown as uses of foreign income. Exports and imports (as a deduction) flow directly into account 1 as components of GDP.

The balancing item, "balance on current account, national income and product accounts," is measured as "current receipts"—U.S. exports of goods and services and income receipts from the rest of the world—less "current payments"—U.S.

imports of goods and services, income payments to the rest of the world, and current taxes and transfer payments to the rest of the world. Current taxes and transfer payments includes taxes paid to foreign governments (less taxes received by the United States from foreigners) and current transfers paid by persons, governments, and businesses. Because the balance on the current account includes the income receipts and payments and current taxes and transfer transactions with the rest of the world, it is a broader measure than the trade deficit (or surplus) of goods and services published jointly each month by the Census Bureau and BEA.

The balance on the current account shows the extent to which current payments to the rest of the world are funded by current receipts; a positive balance suggests that current receipts from the rest of the world exceed current payments to the rest of the world, thereby allowing U.S. residents to lend or acquire other assets abroad. Conversely, any deficit must be funded through borrowing or the disposal of assets. Thus the balance on the current account can be viewed as the acquisition of foreign assets by U.S. residents less the acquisition of U.S. assets by foreign residents.

Account 6. Domestic Capital Account

Line		
1	Gross domestic investment	2,642.9
2	Private fixed investment (1–20).	2,162.5
3	Government fixed investment (1–29)	433.8
4	Change in private inventories (1–25)	46.7
5	Capital account transactions (net) (7–2)	3.9
6	Net lending or net borrowing (–), national income and product accounts (7–3).	–798.0
7	GROSS DOMESTIC INVESTMENT, CAPITAL ACCOUNT TRANSACTIONS, AND NET LENDING	1,848.8
8	Net saving.	251.7
9	Personal saving (3–8).	38.8
10	Undistributed corporate profits with inventory valuation and capital consumption adjustments (2–17)	400.9
11	Wage accruals less disbursements (private) (1–4).	7.5
12	Net government saving (4–10)	–195.4
13	*Plus:* Consumption of fixed capital (1–11)	1,615.2
14	Private ..	1,347.5
15	Government.	267.7
16	General government.	223.6
17	Government enterprises...	44.1
18	*Equals:* Gross saving.	1,866.9
19	Statistical discrepancy (1–13)..	–18.1
20	GROSS SAVING AND STATISTICAL DISCREPANCY	1,848.8

Account 6. Domestic Capital Account

The domestic capital account shows the relationship between saving and investment in the U.S. economy. It can be used to answer key questions about the economy, such as: Are fixed assets being replaced? Is there a shortfall of saving? Which sector shows positive saving? Which sector invests?

The right side of the account shows the sources of saving for the U.S. economy by sector: Personal saving, business saving (specifically, undistributed corporate profits and wage accruals less disbursements), and government saving. The sum of each sector's saving is net saving. Gross saving is net saving plus the consumption of fixed capital. When gross saving is equal to or larger than consumption of fixed capital, the amount of saving is sufficient to cover the aging of fixed assets.

The statistical discrepancy from account 1 appears again in this account. Given the theoretical equality between GDP and GDI, the statistical discrepancy can be viewed as actual (positive or negative) income that is not captured by the data used to measure GDI and, therefore, not distributed to the sectors. Instead, it is shown as a source of (positive or negative) saving in this account, and its addition leads to the summary measure, "gross saving and statistical discrepancy."

The left side of the account reflects the uses of that saving: Gross domestic investment (which reflects investment by private businesses and governments); capital account transactions; and "net lending or net borrowing (–), national income and product accounts." Gross domestic investment—a measure of gross capital formation—is the purchase of new fixed assets plus the change in private inventories. Capital account transactions (net) are cash or in-kind transfer payments to the rest of the world that are linked to the acquisition or disposition of a fixed asset; they provide an indirect measure of the net acquisition of foreign fixed assets by U.S. residents less the net acquisition of U.S. fixed assets by the rest of the world.

The balancing item—net lending or net borrowing (–), national income and product accounts—is shown on the left side of the domestic capital account. When this item is negative, domestic investment cannot be completely funded from the Nation's own saving. When this item is positive, domestic saving is greater than what is needed for the Nation's own investment.

Account 7. Foreign Transactions Capital Account

Line		
1	BALANCE ON CURRENT ACCOUNT, NATIONAL INCOME AND PRODUCT ACCOUNTS (5–20)	–794.1
2	Capital account transactions (net) (6–5).	3.9
3	Net lending or net borrowing (–), national income and product accounts (6–6)	–798.0
4	CAPITAL ACCOUNT TRANSACTIONS (NET) AND NET LENDING, NATIONAL INCOME AND PRODUCT ACCOUNTS	–794.1

Note: Numbers in parentheses indicate accounts and items of counterentry in the accounts. For example, line 5 of account 1 is shown as "Supplements to wages and salaries (3-14)" ; the counterentry is shown in account 3, line 14.

Account 7. Foreign Transactions Capital Account

This account summarizes the capital transactions with the rest of the world that already appear in account 6. While seemingly repetitive, the account shows the counter-entries for those transactions (and thus maintains the "double-entry" characteristic of the summary accounts); additionally, it is useful to separately identify current and capital transactions with the rest of the world in separate accounts.

Derivation of the NIPA Measures

A variety of data sources are used to estimate the NIPA measures. These data sources differ in availability, quality, coverage, and underlying definitions. As a consequence, the timing of the release of estimates and of subsequent revisions is based on the availability of these source data.

Estimate "Vintages"

The data used by BEA are often available only after some lag. In general, the longer the lag time, the better the data are in terms of coverage and detail. Because both quick release and accuracy are highly valued, there is a constant tradeoff between quality and timing. As a result, BEA releases several "vintages" of NIPA estimates for any given quarter or year, with each vintage—or revision—being based on better source data.

"Advance" current quarterly estimates (based on incomplete monthly data), are released near the end of the first month after the end of the quarter. At the end of each of the following two months, revised estimates are released that incorporate revised and newly available monthly and quarterly data; these releases are referred to as "preliminary" and "final" quarterly estimates.

Annual estimates of GDP that are first available as the sum of the quarterly estimates are revised in the "annual revision" each July and in the following two annual revisions. Annual revisions are timed to incorporate newly available annual source data and quarterly data that are released too late to be used in the current quarterly estimates.

The revision cycle culminates, at about 5-year intervals, in a comprehensive revision of the NIPAs. Comprehensive revisions differ from annual revisions in a variety of ways. First, the data used for comprehensive revisions are based in large part on censuses of economic activity, while the monthly, quarterly, and annual data discussed above are generally based on sample surveys. Second, comprehensive revisions have traditionally been used to introduce major improvements in definitions, estimating methods, and data presentations into the accounts. Finally, the estimates may be revised back as far as 1929.

Current-Dollar Estimates

For most NIPA components, the current-dollar estimates are derived from source data that are "value data," where value = price x quantity. Frequently, BEA—which does not collect much of its own data—must adjust the data that are collected by others, primarily government agencies, trade associations, and international organizations.

Most source data are collected for purposes other than the estimation of the NIPAs, and therefore use definitions, population parameters, or time periods that differ from NIPA concepts. Much of the data must be adjusted by filling gaps in coverage or by using available data as proxies for the desired NIPA measure. For periods for which data are not available, NIPA estimates may be derived using existing estimates. For example, when annual data are available and the quarterly are not, the quarterly data are often estimated by interpolation. For the periods beyond those covered by annual estimates (such as the most recent quarter), the quarterly estimates are derived by extrapolation. These interpolations and extrapolations are often based on “indicators”—related data that are used to approximate movements in the NIPA measures.

Quantity and Price Estimates

Changes over time in the current-dollar measures provided in the NIPAs may reflect a change in quantity, a change in price, or a combination of both. For some analyses, it is important to know these separate effects—for instance, to know how much of the change in GDP is due to changes in the quantities of goods and services without the influence of price changes.

Therefore, the NIPAs provide separate estimates of changes in quantities and prices, derived as indexes that provide information on the change from some reference period. BEA describes estimates of quantities as “real” expenditures—for example “real GDP” or “real PCE.” Note that the level of an index in any single period is not in itself meaningful. Instead, it is the relation of that index level to the index level in another period—that is, it is the change in the index over time—that is important. Indeed, the change in real GDP over time is the featured measure of economic activity. In addition, BEA provides measures of the contributions of various components (such as personal consumption expenditures or investment) to GDP growth.

BEA also provides quantity measures in value terms—called chained dollars—by scaling the index. Specifically, the index in the reference year is set equal to the current-dollar level in the same year, and the change in the index in successive and previous periods is multiplied by the current-dollar level to form a time series in monetary terms.

To facilitate the analysis of the drivers of change in the real estimates, BEA provides measures of the con tributions of real components to the percent change in real aggregates. These are provided because the chained-dollar measures of components are not additive, and therefore, accurate measures of a component’s contribution to change cannot be derived from the chained-dollar measures.

References

Approaching a subject as complex as the NIPAs is best done one step at a time. This paper provided the first step; for readers interested in continuing their education, this section offers references, organized by subject area.

Concepts, framework, and history

A Guide to the National Income and Product Accounts. Bureau of Economic Analysis, September 2006. Web site publication. This paper presents background information and a brief history of the NIPAs, and it provides an overview of the definitions, classifications, and statistical conventions underlying the NIPAs.

An Introduction to National Economic Accounting (MP–1): Bureau of Economic Analysis, September 2007. Web site publication. This paper presents an in-depth derivation of the seven account summary of the NIPAs from generalized production, income and outlay, and saving-investment accounts for each sector and shows the links between the NIPAs and business or financial accounting principles.

Concepts and Methods of the U.S. Input-Output Accounts. Bureau of Economic Analysis, September 2006. Web site publication.

Lequiller, Francois and Derek Blades. Understanding National Accounts. Organisation for Economic Co-operation and Development, 2006.

Marcuss, Rosemary D. and Richard E. Kane. "U.S. National Income and Product Statistics: Born of the Great Depression and World War II.' SURVEY OF CURRENT BUSINESS 87 (February 2007): 32–46. This article reviews the early impetus for the development of the accounts.

Estimating Methods and Source Data

"Updated Summary of NIPA Methodologies.' SURVEY 86 (November 2006): 10–27.

Grimm, Bruce T. and Teresa L. Weadock. "Gross Domestic Product: Revisions and Source Data.' SURVEY 86 (February 2006) 11–15.

In addition, numerous SURVEY articles describe annual and comprehensive revisions to the NIPAs. Most recently:

Seskin, Eugene P. and Shelly Smith. "Annual Revision of the National Income and Product Accounts: Annual Estimates for 2004–2006 and Quarterly Estimates for 2004:I–2007:I.' SURVEY 87 (August 2007): 6–29.

Moulton, Brent R. and Eugene P. Seskin. "Preview of the 2003 Comprehensive Revision of the National Income and Product Accounts: Changes in Definitions and Classifications.' SURVEY 83 (June 2003): 17–34.

Mayerhauser, Nicole, Shelly Smith, and David F. Sullivan. "Preview of the 2003 Comprehensive Revision of the National Income and Product Accounts: New and Redesigned Tables.' SURVEY 83 (August 2003): 7–31.

Moylan, Carol E. and Brooks B. Robinson. "Preview of the 2003 Comprehensive Revision of the National Income and Product Accounts: Statistical Changes.' SURVEY 83 (September 2003): 17–32.

Seskin, Eugene P. and Daniel Larkins. "Improved Estimates of the National Income and Product Accounts for 1929–2002: Results of the Comprehensive Revision.' SURVEY 84 (February 2004): 1–29.

Quantity, Price, and Chained-Dollar Indexes

Landefeld, J. Steven, Brent R. Moulton, and Cindy M. Vojtech. "Chained-Dollar Indexes: Issues, Tips on Their Use, and Upcoming Changes.' SURVEY *83* (November 2003): 8–16.

Landefeld, J. Steven and Robert P. Parker. "BEA's Chain Indexes, Time Series, and Measures of Long-Term Economic Growth.' SURVEY 77 (May 1997): 58–68.

Reliability of the Estimates

Fixler, Dennis J. and Bruce T. Grimm. "Reliability of GDP and Related NIPA Estimates.' SURVEY 82 (January 2002): 927.

Fixler, Dennis J. and Bruce T. Grimm. "Reliability of the NIPA Estimates of U.S. Economic Activity.' SURVEY 85 (February 2005): 8–19.

APPENDIX: ACCESSING THE NIPA ESTIMATES INTERACTIVELY

The seven NIPA accounts only summarize the activities described by the full set of NIPA tables.

The NIPA measures appear in much greater detail, (for example, by type of product, by type of expenditure, by sector, by industry, or by function) along with other important aggregates on BEA's Web site at <www.bea.gov>.

NIPA Table Arrangement

The 359 NIPA tables are arranged in roughly the some order as the seven summary accounts. Section 1 of the NIPA tables includes summary income and product tables and other related aggregates. Section 2 includes tables on personal income and outlays. Section 3 includes tables on government receipts and expenditures. Section 4 includes tables on transactions with the rest of the world. Section 5 contains tables on domestic saving and investment. Also included in the full set of NIPA tables, but not shown in the summary accounts, are tables (in section 6) that display estimates of income and employment by industry, tables (in section 7) that feature supplemental economic measures, such as motor vehicle output and housing output, as well as reconciliations of NIPA measures to underlying source data, and tables (in section 8) that contain seasonally unadjusted estimates.

NIPA Table Numbering System

The NIPA tables are numbered so that users can quickly identify the type of estimate (such as current dollars, quantity indexes, and percent changes) shown in each table. Table numbers are in the format “X.Y.Z,” where “X” indicates the NIPA table section, “Y” indicates the table number in the section, and “Z” indicates the type of estimate presented. The system is outlined below:

Table	Estimate Description
X.Y.1	Percent change from preceding period in real estimates
X.Y.2	Contributions to percent change in real estimates
X.Y.3	Real estimates, quantity indexes
X.Y.4	Price indexes
X.Y.5	Current dollars
X.Y.6	Real estimates, chained dollars
X.Y.7	Percent change in prices
X.Y.8	Contributions to percent change in prices
X.Y.9	Implicit price deflators
X.Y.10	Percentage shares of GDP

Example

To retrieve data on the percent changes in real consumer spending over time from BEA's Web site, www.bea.gov>, begin by clicking on "National," then "Interactive NIPA tables," and finally "list of all NIPA tables."

Consumer spending, or personal consumption expenditures (PCE), is a component of the personal income and outlay account. Therefore, select "2" from the "list of all NIPA tables" page:

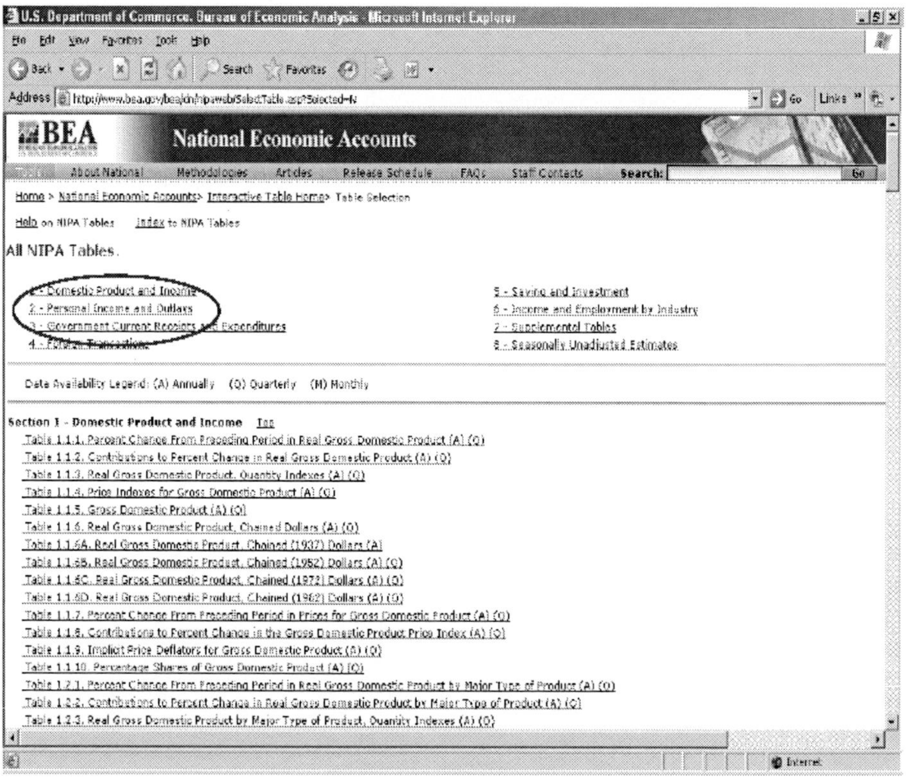

From the list of section 2 tables, detailed PCE estimates are found in the NIPA table family 2.3. From the NIPA table numbering system described above, percent changes in real PCE are found in tables ending in 1. Therefore, one would select NIPA table 2.3.1:

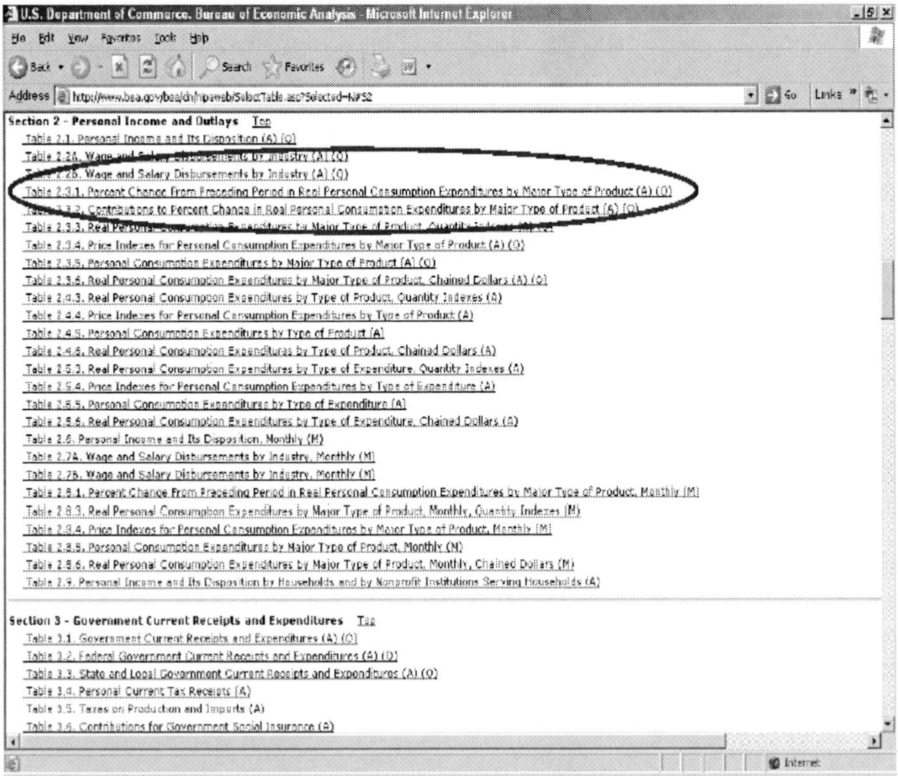

The interactive NIPA tables can be customized to meet a user's specific needs. The "data table options" bar allows one to select the time period and the frequency (annuals, quarters, and in some cases, months) of the data. Note that the quarterly and monthly estimates are both seasonally adjusted and annualized.

Seasonal adjustment removes variations that occur in the same month or quarter every year so that the remaining movements in the series better reflect trends in economic activity. Annualized growth rates are published to facilitate comparisons between estimates of different frequencies.

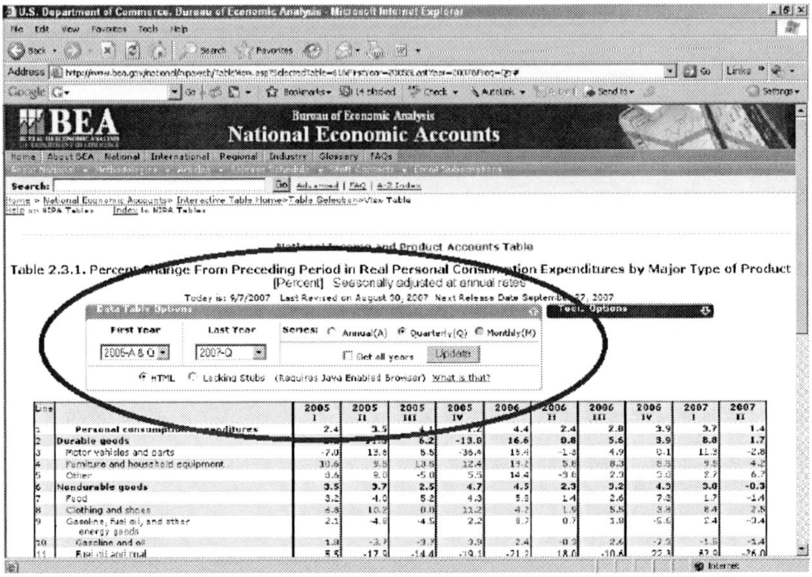

Scrolling down to the bottom of the table, one is presented with several options for downloading the data: Additionally, there are options available that allow you to print directly from the Web.

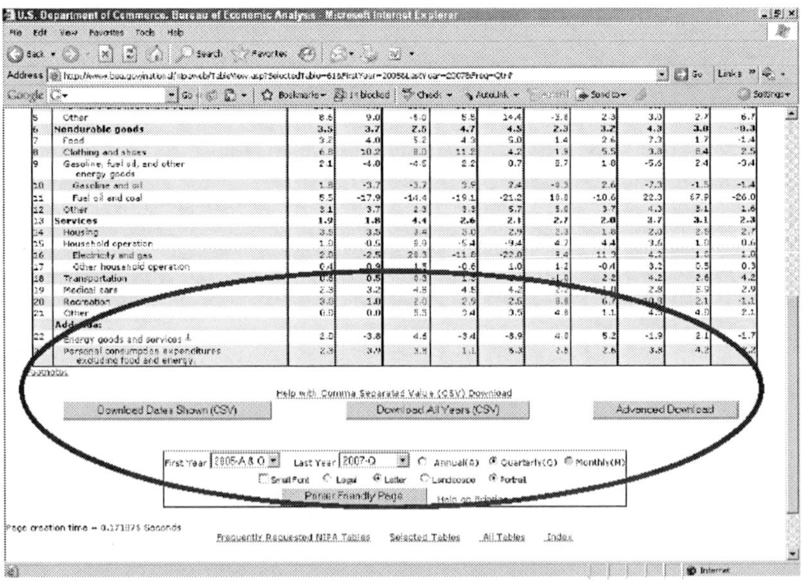

In: Measuring the Economy: GDP and NIPAs ISBN: 978-1-60741-199-4
Editor: Kemal Sahin © 2009 Nova Science Publishers, Inc.

Chapter 2

METHODOLOGY PAPERS: U.S. NATIONAL INCOME AND PRODUCT ACCOUNTS*

Carlos M. Gutierrez, Cynthia A. Glassman, J. Steven Landefeld and Rosemary D. Marcuss

ACKNOWLEDGMENTS

Part I, "Overview of the NIPAs," was prepared by Stephanie H. McCulla, an Economist in the National Income and Wealth Division at the Bureau of Economic Analysis (BEA).

Part II, "Underlying Economic Accounts"; Part III, "Economic Accounts for Sectors"; and Part IV, "NIPA Summary Accounts"; were prepared by Charles Ian Mead, an Economist in the Office of the Director at BEA.

Brent R. Moulton, Associate Director for National Economic Accounts at BEA, provided overall supervision for the preparation of this project.

---

* This is an edited, excerpted and augmented edition of a Bureau of Economic Analysis, U.S. Department of Commerce publication.

PREFACE

This paper provides a comprehensive explanation of the conceptual basis and framework of the U.S. national income and product accounts (NIPAs). It describes the structure and purpose of the U.S. economic accounts, discusses the relationship between business and financial accounting and national economic accounting, and presents a derivation of the seven NIPA summary accounts from generalized production, income and outlay, and capital accounts for each sector of the economy.

This paper updates and replaces “An Introduction to National Economic Accounting” (MP1), which was published in March 1985.

Comments about this paper are invited. Please contact the BEA National Economic Accounts Directorate, 1441 L St. NW, BE–6, Washington, DC 20230 or by e-mail at <GDPniwd@BEA.gov>.

THE national income and product accounts (NIPAs) produced by the Bureau of Economic Analysis (BEA) have become a mainstay of modern macroeconomic analysis for the U.S. economy. In fact, the Commerce Department in 2000 named the NIPAs, and their marquee measure, gross domestic product (GDP), “its achievement of the century.”[1] Because these accounts provide a detailed picture of economic activity at a given time, as well as a consistently defined series of measures over time, they are indispensable to researchers, forecasters, government officials, academics, and investors who use them for a wide array of academic, public policy, and other purposes.

Given the importance of the NIPAs, users often seek a detailed explanation of the concepts that underlie them. The goal of this methodology paper is to present the conceptual basis and framework of the U.S. NIPAs.[2] Specifically, the paper demonstrates how the seven accounts that summarize the NIPAs are derived from conventional accounting statements—in particular, the balance sheet, income statements, and the statement of cash flow familiar to business accounting. In deriving the summary accounts, the paper also illustrates how they reflect the activity occurring within the entire economy.[3]

I. OVERVIEW OF THE NIPAS

The NIPAs are a set of economic accounts that provide detailed measures of the value and composition of national output and the incomes generated in the production of that output. Essentially, the NIPAs provide a detailed snapshot of the myriad transactions that make up the economy—buying and selling goods and services, hiring of labor, investing, renting property, paying taxes, and the like. More specifically, the seven summary accounts of the NIPAs simplify both the transactors and transactions in the economy. The transactors of the domestic economy are grouped into three distinct groups, or sectors—persons, businesses, and government; a fourth sector for the rest of the world is added to cover transactions between the Nation and foreigners. The seven summary accounts of the NIPAs show the contribution of each sector to the output of the economy, their income and outlays, and their saving and investment.

The best-known NIPA measure is GDP, which is defined as the market value of the goods and services produced by labor and property located in the United States. The NIPAs calculate GDP as the sum of familiar final expenditure components: Personal consumption expenditures, private investment, government spending (consumption and investment) and net exports. However, GDP is just one of many economic measures presented in the NIPAs, which include seven summary accounts and nearly 300 tables of supporting data.

National Economic Accounts System

The NIPAs are part of an integrated system of national economic accounts that also includes the industry accounts and the flow of funds accounts. BEA's industry accounts consist of the input-output (I-O) accounts, which trace the flow of goods and services among industries in the production process and which show the value added by each industry and the detailed commodity composition of national output, and the GDP by industry accounts, which measure the contribution of each private industry and of government to GDP.[4]

The Federal Reserve Board's flow of funds accounts record the value of tangible and financial assets acquired and the value of liabilities incurred throughout the U.S. economy, and the sources of the funds used to acquire the assets.[5]

In addition, BEA prepares two other sets of U.S. economic accounts: The international accounts, which consist of the international transactions (balance of payments) accounts and the international investment position accounts; and the regional accounts, which consist of the estimates of GDP by state, of state personal income, and of local area personal income. Finally, the Bureau of Labor Statistics prepares estimates of productivity for the U.S. economy (which are partially based on estimates of GDP). Altogether, the system of U.S. economic accounts presents a coherent, comprehensive, and consistent picture of U.S. economic activity.

An internationally accepted conceptual framework for these accounts is found in the System of National Accounts 1993 (SNA). The SNA provides a set of guidelines for national statistical offices compiling national economic accounts. Along with national accountants from many countries, BEA actively participated in developing these guidelines.

Many of the major improvements made to the NIPAs in recent years are consistent with the guidelines provided by the SNA. These include the adoption of chain-type quantity and price indexes, the capitalization of software, and the recognition of the implicit services provided by commercial banks. BEA is currently participating in the international effort to update these guidelines to take account of changes in the economic environment.[6]

The remainder of this section discusses the concepts underlying the NIPAs.

Estimating Concepts and Conventions

Production Boundary

One of the fundamental questions that must be addressed in preparing national economic accounts is how to define the production boundary—that is, what parts of the myriad human activities are to be included in or excluded from the measure of the economy's production. According to the SNA, "Economic production may be defined as an activity carried out under the control and responsibility of an institutional unit that uses inputs of labor, capital, and goods and services to produce outputs of goods or services. There must be an institutional unit that assumes responsibility for the process and owns any goods produced as outputs or is entitled to be paid, or otherwise compensated, for the services provided."[7]

Under this definition, certain natural processes may be included in or excluded from production, depending upon whether they are under the ownership or control of an entity in the economy. For example, the growth of trees in an uncultivated forest is not included in production, but the harvesting of the trees from that forest is included.

The general definition of the production boundary may then be restricted by functional considerations. In the SNA (and in the U.S. accounts), certain household activities—such as housework, do-it-yourself projects, and care of family members—are excluded, partly because by nature these activities tend to be self-contained and have limited impact on the rest of the economy and because their inclusion could diminish the usefulness of the accounts for long-standing analytical purposes, such as business cycle analysis.[8]

In the NIPAs, the production boundary is further restricted by practical considerations about whether the productive activity can be accurately valued or measured. For example, illegal activities, such as gambling and prostitution in some states, should in principle be included in measures of production. However, these activities are excluded from the U.S. accounts because they are by their very nature conducted out of sight of public scrutiny and so data are not available to measure them.

Finally, the production boundary is sometimes altered in order to accommodate innovations and structural changes in the economy. For example, in the 1999 comprehensive revision of the NIPAs, the value of U.S. production was increased by a change in definition that recognized business and government expenditures for software as fixed investment rather than as intermediate purchases for business and as consumption expenditures for government.[9]

Market Value

Goods and services in the NIPAs are measured at market prices; the value of output is equal to the market price of the good or service times the quantity of the good or service produced during the year. In cases where market prices do not fully reflect the value of a good or service or where services are provided without an actual exchange, the value of the good or service produced may be "imputed" from similar market transactions, as described below. In cases where there are no similar market transactions available to impute a value, such as for goods or services that are provided for free (or at insignificant prices) by government and nonprofit institutions, the market price is estimated based on the costs of production.

Imputations

Imputations are made to include in the accounts the value of certain goods and services that have no observable price and are often not associated with any observable transaction.[10]

For example, in their role as an intermediary between borrowers and lenders, banks provide services for which they do not charge an explicit price. However, they are compensated for these services through the payment of higher interest rates by borrowers and the receipt of lower interest rates by savers. To keep GDP invariant to whether or not a price is explicit or implicit, the value of the service reflected by such exchanges is imputed. Imputations are also made to keep GDP invariant to institutional arrangements. For example, unlike the provision for payment of housing services to a renter by a landlord, the provision of housing services to an occupant that owns the housing does not involve an exchange between two or more transactors. However, excluding the value of such services would cause variations in GDP that would depend only on variations in institutional arrangements. Therefore, the NIPAs include an imputation of the value of the services provided by owner-occupied housing.[11]

Final Versus Intermediate Products

In the NIPAs, production represents unduplicated output. That is, GDP is designed to avoid double counting the value of goods and services that are inputs into the production of other goods and services and that are not used in future production. These intermediate inputs are already reflected in the market value of the final product and are therefore excluded so that the measure of output is an unduplicated total. This is done using either the final expenditures approach or the value added approach, as described below.

Alternative Approaches to Measuring GDP

GDP measures output as the "market value of final goods and services"—that is, as the sum of personal consumption expenditures, gross private domestic investment, government consumption expenditures and gross investment, and net exports of goods and services. This is known as the "expenditures" or "product side" approach to measuring GDP. Another way to measure GDP is as the sum of the charges generated in the production of the final goods and services. Because the market price of a final good or service reflects all the charges associated with producing that good or service, an "income-side" measure of output, gross domestic income (GDI), can be derived as the sum of the charges against production. Specifically, GDI is measured as the sum of compensation of employees (the return to labor), taxes on production less subsidies (a nonincome charge against production), net operating surplus (the net return to capital and entrepreneurship), and consumption of fixed capital (the using up of capital).

In theory, GDP and GDI are equal. In practice, the differences in the data used to derive the two measures lead to a discrepancy. This "statistical discrepancy" is defined in the NIPAs as GDP less GDI. Because the source data used to derive product-side measures of output are based on more comprehensive surveys and censuses, BEA considers them more reliable. Therefore, the statistical discrepancy appears as a component on the income side of the account.

Another way to measure output, used by BEA's I-O accounts, is known as the "value added" approach. In these accounts, value added is defined as the difference between an industry's total output—that is, its sales plus the change in inventories arising from production—and its intermediate purchases from other industries. When value added is aggregated across all industries in the economy, industry sales to and purchases from each other cancel out, and the remainder is industry sales to final users, or GDP.[12]

Geographic Coverage

In the NIPAs, and in the I-O accounts, the "U.S. estimates" cover the 50 states and the District of Columbia. This treatment aligns GDP with other U.S. statistics, such as population and employment. Transactions between the United States and Puerto Rico, the U.S. territories, and the Northern Mariana Islands are included in the "rest-of-the-world" sector.[13]

In the NIPAs, a distinction is made between "domestic" measures and "national" measures. Domestic measures cover activities that take place within the geographic borders of the United States. For example, GDP measures the value of goods and services produced by labor and capital located in the United States. In contrast, national measures cover activities that are performed using resources supplied by U.S. residents.[14] For example, gross national product (GNP) measures the value of goods and services produced by labor and capital supplied by U.S. residents. Thus, for an assembly plant that is owned by a U.S. auto company and located in Great Britain, a portion of the value of its output is included in GNP, but none of its output is included in GDP. And, for an assembly plant that is owned by a Japanese auto company and located in the United States, all of its output is included in GDP, but only a portion of its output is included in GNP.

Capital, Investment, and Depreciation

Economic production as defined above covers all final goods and services produced during a given period. Nondurable goods and services are generally consumed fully within a year. In contrast, durable goods—such as equipment and software—and structures provide services over longer periods of time. In the NIPAs, purchases of new durable goods and structures by businesses or government for use in production are treated as gross fixed investment, as are purchases of new residential housing. Purchases of durable goods by individuals, on the other hand, are treated as consumption in the NIPAs, rather than as investment, in accordance with the NIPA convention that nonmarket household production is outside the scope of GDP.[15]

Both consumption and investment contribute to GDP in the NIPAs, but the distinction is important because investment implies a stock of fixed assets, or capital, which in turn implies depreciation, or a decline in the value of the stock of capital over time.[16]

More specifically, depreciation, or the consumption of fixed capital, is defined as the deductions from the capital stock over the period due to age, wear and tear, accidental damage, and obsolescence. Thus, depreciation is a charge against production—that is, it reflects an amount that would need to be set aside to eventually replace fixed assets as they are used up in the production process—and is therefore a component of the NIPAs income-side measure of output. Its inclusion in GDI ensures that the measure fully reflects the income- side value of final goods and services, but it also suggests that the measure overstates the capabilities of the economy to produce goods and services for consumption or to add to the capital stock. Thus, "net" measures that are provided in the NIPAs—that is, measures that exclude depreciation, such as net domestic product (NDP) and net domestic investment—are preferred for many analyses. Nevertheless, GDP remains the most commonly cited statistic of the overall level of economic activity.

Inventories

A key component of investment, and thus GDP, is the change in private inventories, which reflects the value of goods that have been produced but not yet sold. For a given period, additions to inventories reflect production in that period and so are included in GDP, while withdrawals from inventories reflect production in past periods and so are excluded from GDP.

In the NIPAs, additions to, less withdrawals from, inventories is measured as ending period less beginning period inventories and recorded as a single item, "change in inventories."

II. Underlying Economic Accounts

Many of the important concepts that are used in the NIPAs can be understood by relating a theoretical set of economic accounts for a business firm to its financial statements. This section will briefly review fundamental accounting principles and common financial statements before illustrating how they relate to the NIPAs.

Fundamental Accounting Principles

The formal practice of financial accounting has a much longer history than that of national economic accounting.[17] Thus, it is no surprise that national economic accounting is based on many of the same fundamental principles that were first adopted in financial accounting. However, differences between the two fields still exist as each serves a separate purpose.

The purpose of financial accounting is to provide a set of financial statements that convey information on the financial position, the results of operations, and the manner in which cash flows through an individual business. The financial position includes the resources available to a business (assets), the claims of creditors on these resources (liabilities), and the claims of business owners on these resources (owners' equity). The results of operations include the income received by a business (revenue), the costs incurred while earning this income (expenses), and the profits earned by a business (net earnings).

One of the most fundamental principles used in both financial and national economic accounting is double-entry bookkeeping. In double-entry bookkeeping, activities that affect the resources available to a business are reflected at least twice in a general ledger: At least once on the right side as a source of financing (credit) and at least once on the left side as a use of financing (debit). The advantage of double-entry bookkeeping is that it provides a means to validate the values entered into a general ledger because the sum of entries on each side should equal.

Double-entry bookkeeping in national economic accounting has a somewhat different role than double- entry bookkeeping in financial accounting. The national accounts are designed to measure all transactions in the economy from the perspective of both participants in a transaction—for example, both the buyer and the seller. Each transaction is recorded as a payment by one sector and a receipt by another—for example, corporate income tax is a payment by a corporation and a receipt of the government.[18] This system not only provides a means to validate the values entered into a set of national economic accounts, but it also provides alternative ways to calculate a measure when a complete set of information is not available for one of the sectors that is involved in a set of exchanges.

Another fundamental principle used in both financial and national economic accounting is that related revenues and expenses must be recorded during the same accounting period. To ensure this, the accrual accounting method is usually used. This method records the sale of goods or assets when ownership passes, the sale of services when they are provided, the generation of output when goods and services are produced, and the consumption of intermediate goods and services when they are used. The accrual accounting method differs from the cash accounting method, which records revenues when cash is actually received and expenses when cash is actually paid.

In financial accounting, assets and depreciation are commonly (but not invariably) valued at historical costs, which are the actual prices that were paid in their acquisition. Historical costs are commonly used in financial accounting because they are regarded as relatively objective, since they are supported by verifiable historical transactions, and relatively conservative, since they do not include holding gains (or losses) that have not been realized.[19]

In national economic accounting, assets and depreciation are valued at current costs, which are the actual or estimated market prices that prevail at the time assets are valued or depreciation occurs. Current costs are used in national economic accounting because they serve as the best practical approximation to the economic notion of opportunity costs. Opportunity costs are the foregone benefits that could have been secured with the next best alternative use of a resource, which serves as one of the most fundamental concepts used in economic analysis.

Common Financial Statements

The two principal statements that summarize the activities that are recorded in the general ledger of a business are the balance sheet and the income statement. Although the form of these statements often differs across businesses, their purposes are the same. A balance sheet shows the financial position of a business at a given point in time. An income statement shows the operating results of a business during an accounting period between two balance sheets.

Two additional statements are usually required to supplement the information provided on the balance sheet and income statement. The first, a statement of cash flows, shows how cash streams through a business during an accounting period. Its purpose is to allow for an assessment of a business' ability to settle liabilities, pay dividends, and respond favorably to unanticipated events. The second, a statement of owners' equity, shows how the claims of owners on the assets of a business change during an accounting period. Its purpose is to show how the change in retained earnings between two consecutive balance sheets is related to net earnings. Sometimes this demonstration occurs at the end of an income statement, in which case, the result is presented as a single statement of income and retained earnings.

The rest of this section introduces the financial statements of a representative business firm and then derives the set of economic accounts that underlie the NIPAs.

Balance Sheet

The basic identity underlying the balance sheet is that the business firm's assets less its liabilities are equal to owners' equity—that is,

Assets – liabilities = owners' equity.

Since owners' equity is conceptually the residual claim of the corporation's owners on assets once all liabilities have been met, its value is simply equal to the value of the corporation's assets less the value of its liabilities. Thus, if total assets increase without an offsetting increase in total liabilities, then owners' equity rises; if total assets decrease without an offsetting decrease in total liabilities, then owners' equity falls.

On the balance sheet, there are several categories of assets, liabilities, and owners' equity, which is called stockholders' equity in the case of a corporation (table 1).

Current Assets

These are resources that are usually converted into cash or used within the period of a year.[20] They include cash and cash equivalents, accounts receivable, inventories, and short-term investments. Cash and cash equivalents include coins, currency, and undeposited checks; money orders; demand deposits at banks; and certain highly liquid investments. Accounts receivable are short-term credits that have been extended to customers to cover goods and services that the corporation has already provided but for which payment has not yet been received. These credits are included on the balance sheet because related revenue and expenses need to be reflected during the same accounting period. Short-term investments consist of other types of assets, such as securities of other corporations, that are expected to be converted back into cash within the time period that is used to define current assets.

Fixed Assets

These consist of assets that are used in a productive capacity, have physical substance, are relatively long-lived, and provide future benefits that are readily measurable. They mainly consist of plant, equipment, and land, and they are usually valued at historical costs less accumulated depreciation.

Long-Term Investments

These consist of financial assets, such as securities of other corporations, that are expected to be converted into cash or used after the period of time that is used to measure current assets.

Current Liabilities

These consist of obligations that are either due upon demand or expected to be due within the same period of time that is used to define current assets. Current liabilities include accounts payable and short-term liabilities, such as the principal that must be paid during the current period on long-term debts. Accounts payable are short-term debts that have been assumed by the business for goods and services already received but for which payment has not yet been made.

Table 1. Balance Sheet, December 31, 20__(In thousands)

Assets	
Current assets:	
Cash and cash equivalents..	280
Accounts receivable.	300
Inventories	10
Short-term assets	10
Total current assets.	600
Fixed assets.	1,390
Long-term investments	190
Total assets .	2,180
Liabilities and stockholders' equity	
Current liabilities:	
Accounts payable..	200
Short-term liabilities	70
Total current liabilities.	270
Long-term liabilities	310
Stockholders' equity:	
Capital stock	260
Assets	
Retained earnings	1,340
Total stockholders' equity.	1,600
Total liabilities and stockholders' equity.	2,180

Long-Term Liabilities

These consist of long-term obligations, such as note and bond payments, that are not expected to be due until after the period of time that is used to define current liabilities.

Stockholders' Equity

The ownership stake of stockholders includes the amount shareholders paid for their stocks (capital stock) and the retained earnings of the corporation. Retained earnings are net earnings that have been saved by the corporation for future use or investment.

Income and Retained Earnings

The basic identity underlying the statement of income and retained earnings is that the business firm's net earnings are equal to its revenue less its expenses—that is,

Net earnings = revenue – expenses.

However, the statement does not derive net earnings by subtracting all expenses from all revenue in a single step. Rather, it derives net income through a series of steps to provide a useful set of intermediate income measures to investors and creditors.

Gross Profits

This measure is derived by subtracting the costs of goods and services sold from sales, which are measured net of discounts and returns (table 2). Although various accounting conventions may be used to record the costs of goods and services sold, the purpose of this measure is to account for the costs that can be directly linked to the production of goods and services.[21] These expenses include purchases of intermediate goods and services, labor costs of production workers, depreciation of plants and equipment used in production, and changes in inventories (beginning-ofperiod less end-of-period).

Table 2. Statement of Income and Retained Earnings, For Year Ending December 31, 20__(In thousands)

Sales, net of discounts and returns	2,630
Costs of goods and services sold	(1,770)
Gross profits	860
Operating expenses	(460)
Operating income.	400
Other income	10
Net earnings before interest and taxes .	410
Interest receipts.	10
Interest payments.	(20)
Net earnings before taxes	400
Income taxes	(150)
Net earnings after taxes	250
Dividends paid.	(110)
Additions to retained earnings	140

Operating Income

This measure is derived by subtracting operating expenses and depreciation from gross profits. Operating expenses consist of the costs that are associated with the general operations of the corporation but cannot be directly linked to the production of goods and services. These expenses include labor costs of administrative staff, property taxes, depreciation of office buildings and equipment, inspection fees, charitable contributions, and royalty payments.

Other Income

This consists of income that is received from activities that are not associated with normal business activities, such as gains (net of losses) on sales of securities and fixed assets.

Net Earnings before Interest and Taxes

This measure is derived by adding other income to operating income.

Net Earnings after Taxes

This measure is derived by adding interest receipts, subtracting interest payments, and then subtracting income taxes from net earnings before interest and taxes.

Additions to Retained Earnings

This measure is derived by subtracting dividends paid to shareholders from net earnings after taxes.

Cash Flows

The statement of cash flows begins by separately deriving the net cash flows associated with the operating, investing, and financial activities of the corporation (table 3). Afterwards, these three measures are summed to arrive at the net increase in cash.

Table 3. Statement of Cash Flows, For Year Ending December 31, 20__(In thousands)

Cash flows from operating activities:	
Net earnings after taxes..	250
Adjustments to reconcile net earnings after taxes to cash	
provided by operating activities:	
Depreciation of plant and equipment .	170
Changes in assets and liabilities:	
Increase in current assets.	30)
Decrease in current liabilities.	10
Net cash provided by operating activities	400
Cash flows from investing activities:	
Sales of fixed assets .	10
Sales of securities.	0
Purchases of fixed assets .	(100)
Purchases of securities	(30)
Net cash used in investment activities	(120)
Cash flows from financing activities:	
Issues of bonds.	40
Issues of capital stock	50
Retirements of bonds.	(120)
Dividend payments	(110)
Net cash used in financing activities.	(140)
Net increase in cash .	140
Cash and cash equivalents at beginning of year	140
Cash and cash equivalents at end of year .	280

Note: Negative numbers in a running total are shown in parentheses.

Net Cash Flows Provided by Operating Activities

This measure is indirectly derived by applying a series of adjustments to the accrual-based measure of net earnings after taxes to arrive at the cash-based measure of net cash flows.[22] These adjustments include adding depreciation, subtracting increases in current assets, and adding decreases in current liabilities.

Net Cash Flows Used in Investment Activities

This measure is directly derived by subtracting cash outflows from cash inflows. Cash inflows in this section of the statement include sales of fixed assets, along with sales of securities that have been issued by other corporations. Cash outflows in this section of the statement include purchases of fixed assets, along with purchases of securities that have been issued by other corporations.

Net Cash Flows Used in Financing Activities

This measure is directly derived by subtracting cash outflows from cash inflows. Cash inflows in this section of the statement include the issuance of bonds and securities. Cash outflows in this section of the statement include the retirement of bonds and dividends paid to stockholders.

FINANCIAL STATEMENTS, ECONOMIC ACCOUNTS FOR THE BUSINESS SECTOR, AND THE NIPAS

The three financial statements discussed above are related to four economic accounts that provide the building blocks for the key measures of the business sector in the NIPAs.

The first economic account, a production account, shows the contribution that is made by the business firm to GDP. The second account, an enterprise income account, shows how net income from production and income from the ownership of financial assets is used to fund the payment of interest to the business firm's creditors. The third account, an income and outlay account, shows how the business income that remains after interest and certain types of transfer payments have been made is either retained by the business firm or used to pay income taxes to the government or dividends to the business firm's owners. The fourth account, a capital account, shows how the retained income of the business is used to purchase fixed assets.

All four of these economic accounts can be conceptually derived from the information in the business firm's financial statements. In particular, the first three of these accounts are directly related to the statement of income and retained earnings. The last of these accounts is directly related to the portion of the statement of cash flows that deals with fixed assets and depreciation.

The derivation of each economic account from the financial statements of the business firm can be easily seen by first creating a ledger that organizes transactions into measures that appear in each of the respective accounts (table 4). Afterwards, national accounting identities are used to define the accounts, and few of the items in the ledger are adjusted or moved to the other side of the account to create the final measures.

Table 4. Detailed Ledger for Sources and Uses of Revenue, For year ending December 31, 20__(In thousands)

Uses		Sources	
Charges against revenue in the production account:		Revenue in the production account: Sales, net of discounts 1	2,740
Compensation of employees	1,610		
Wages and salaries	1,380		
Supplements to wages and salaries.	230		
Purchases of intermediate goods and services.	400		
Changes in inventories	10		
Taxes on production and imports 1	160		
Depreciation	170		
Charges against revenue in the enterprise income account:		Revenue in the enterprise income account:	
Interest and miscellaneous payments	20	Interest receipts	10
Current transfer payments (net).	10	Dividend receipts	20
Charges against revenue in the income and outlay account:			
Taxes on corporate income	150		
Dividend payments	110		
Undistributed corporate profits 2 .	130		
Charges against revenue	2,770	Revenue	2,770

Production Account for a Business Firm

The production account for a business firm shows the value of goods and services that can be attributed to the business firm both directly in terms of the goods and services that it produces and indirectly in terms of the costs that it incurs during production (first panel of table 5).

Table 5. Economic Accounts for a Corporation, For year ending December 31, 20__(In thousands)

Production Account			
Uses		Sources	
Compensation of employees	1,610	Gross output.	2,730
Wages and salaries	1,380	Sales	2,740
Supplements to wages and salaries.	230	Changes in inventories..	(10)
Taxes on production and imports.	160	*Less:* Intermediate goods and services	400
Depreciation	170		
Net operating surplus	390		
Charges against gross value added and net operating surplus	2,330	Gross value added	2,330
Enterprise Income Account			
Uses		Sources	
Interest and miscellaneous payments	20	Net operating surplus.	390
Current transfer payments	10	Income receipts on assets	30
Corporate profits..	390	Interest .	10
		Dividend receipts	20
Uses of income and corporate profits.	420	Sources of income	420
Income and Outlay Account			
Uses		Sources	
Taxes on corporate income .	150	Corporate profits	390
Equals: Profits after tax .	240		
Dividend payments	110		
Undistributed corporate profits	130		
Distributions of income and undistributed corporate profits	390	Sources of income	390
Capital Account			
Uses		Sources	
Gross investment.	90	Gross saving	300
Net acquisition less disposal of non-produced nonfinancial assets...	10	Undistributed corporate profits..	130
Net lending or net borrowing	210	Depreciation	170
		Net capital transfers	10
Gross investment, net acquisition less disposal of nonproduced nonfinancial assets, and net lending	310	Gross saving and net capital transfers	310

The basic identity underlying the production account is that gross value added is equal to the charges against gross value added and net operating surplus—that is,

Gross value added = charges against gross value added + net operating surplus.

Net operating surplus, which is a profits-like measure, is conceptually the balance on the account that remains once the charges against gross value added have been deducted from gross value added. Thus, if gross value added increases without an offsetting increase in charges against gross value added, then net operating surplus will rise; if gross value added de- creases without an offsetting decrease in charges against gross value added, then net operating surplus will fall.

Gross output, which appears on the right side of the account, is derived by moving the changes in inventories to the right side of the ledger, with a change in sign so that it represents end-of-period inventories less beginning-of-period inventories, and adding its value to sales.[23] Gross value added is derived by moving intermediate goods and services to the right side of the ledger and subtracting its value from gross output. Charges against gross value added, which appear on the left side of the account, consist of the compensation of employees, taxes on production and imports, and depreciation.

A few additional points about the measures in this account should be made.

Changes in Inventories

This measure differs from that shown in the financial statements of corporations because it is based on the current costs that are used in national accounting rather than the historic costs that are often used in financial accounting.

Changes in inventories are moved to the right side of the account because what is sold by the corporation is often not equal to what is produced during the same accounting period. In particular, if the firm produces more goods than it sells, then the remaining goods are placed into inventories; if the firm produces fewer goods than it sells, then the shortfall is met by withdrawing goods from inventories. The addition of the changes in inventories to sales removes sales of goods that were not produced during the current period and adds produced goods that were not sold during the current period to arrive at a true measure of gross output during the period.

Compensation of Employees

This measure, which appears on the left side of the account, consists of the sum of a measure of wages and salaries and a measure for supplements to wages and salaries. Wages and salaries are broadly defined to include commissions, tips, and bonuses; voluntary employee contributions to deferred compensation plans, such as 401(k) plans; employee gains from exercising stock options; and receipts-in-kind that represent income. Supplements to wages and salaries consist of employer contributions to employee pension and insurance plans and of employer contributions for government social insurance.

Taxes on Production and Imports

These taxes consist of tax liabilities that are incurred in the production of goods and services. They include Federal excise taxes and customs duties and state and local sales taxes, property taxes, motor vehicle licenses, severance taxes, other taxes, and special assessments. All of these items except for sales and excise taxes are included in the measure of operating expenses in the business firm's financial statements. Sales and excise taxes are included in the measure of taxes on production and imports because their value is added to sales on the other side of the ledger so that GDP is valued at the costs to final purchasers.

Consumption of Fixed Capital (CFC)

This measure replaces the measures of depreciation in the individual business accounts. Although the two measures are closely related, they differ in two important ways. First, CFC is based on a consistent set of service lives and empirically based depreciation schedules rather than on the various conventions that are used in financial accounting. Second, CFC is based on the current costs that are used in national accounting rather than the historical costs that are often used in financial accounting.[24]

Net Operating Surplus

This measure is defined as the residual claim against gross value added after the charges directly related to production—that is, compensation of employees, taxes on production and imports (less subsidies), and consumption of fixed capital—have been deducted. It measures the surplus or deficit accruing from production before taking account of any interest and dividends receivable on financial assets owned by the corporation; payments to those with financial claims on the firm, such as interest or dividends payable; and other nonoperating payments, such as current business transfer payments and taxes on corporate income.

The net operating surplus reflects the net return to assets that the firm uses in production.

Enterprise Income Account

The enterprise income account shows how the corporation's operating surplus and its nonoperating income (interest and dividends) are used for interest payments to the providers of financial capital and for transfer payments, leaving a balance for the owners as corporate profits (second panel of table 5).

The basic identity underlying the enterprise income account is that the sources of income are equal to uses of income and corporate profits—that is,

Sources of income = uses of income + corporate profits.

Corporate profits are conceptually the residual charge against income that remains after uses of income have been deducted.

On the right side of the account, the sources of income consist of both the net income from production and income receipts on assets. Net income from production is measured by net operating surplus, which has been carried over from the production account. Income receipts on assets consist of interest receipts from other economic institutions and of dividend receipts.

On the left side of the account, uses of net income consist of interest and miscellaneous payments and of current transfer payments. A few points should be made about the transactions and adjustments that are included in these measures.

Interest Receipts

This measure differs from that used in financial accounting because it includes both the monetary receipts that are recorded on financial statements and the imputed receipts that are used in national economic accounting. These imputed interest receipts are included to account for the value of implicit financial services that are provided by commercial banks and by property and casualty insurance companies.[25]

Interest and Miscellaneous Payments

This measure differs from the measure of interest payments used in financial accounting in two ways. First it includes any rents or royalties for natural resources paid to government that may be included in the measure of operating surplus in the business firm's financial statements. Rents and royalties related to other items, such as building equipment, or patented research, are excluded from this measure because they are treated as purchases of intermediate goods and services. Second, much like the measure of interest receipts in this account, interest and miscellaneous payments includes imputed interest payments to account for the value of implicit financial services that are provided by commercial banks and by property and casualty insurance companies.

Current Transfer Payments (Net)

These payments consist of cash or in-kind payments where nothing is received in return. However, current transfer payments exclude payments that are related to acquisition or disposal of fixed assets, such as capital gains or estate or gift taxes. These types of transfers are classified as capital transfers and included in the capital account. For the business firm, current transfer payments include fines and certain fees paid to government, the portion of insurance premiums that is not a payment for service (net of benefits received), charitable contributions to nonprofit organizations, and various other unrequited payments. With the exception of the adjusted value for insurance premiums, these items are included as in the measure of operating expenses in the firm's financial statements.

Corporate Profits

The measure of corporate profits includes adjustments so that it is based on the inventory valuation and depreciation concepts that are used in national economic accounting.[26]

Income and Outlay Account

The income and outlay account shows how corporate profits, which have been carried forward from the enterprise income account, are used to either pay corporate income taxes or dividends to shareholders or are retained by the corporation (third panel of table 5).

The basic identity underlying the income and outlay account is that the sources of income are equal to the distributions of income and undistributed corporate profits—that is,

Sources of income = distributions of income + undistributed corporate profits.

Undistributed corporate profits are the residual charge against income that remains once distributions of income have been made to other economic agents.

Capital Account

The capital account shows how saving is used to acquire nonfinancial assets, such as fixed assets and inventories (fourth panel of table 5).

The basic identity underlying the capital account is that the value of gross savings and net capital transfers is equal to the value of gross investment and the value of net lending or borrowing—that is,

Gross saving and net capital transfers = gross investment + acquisition less disposal of nonproduced nonfinancial assets + net lending or borrowing.

Net lending or borrowing is the residual claim on gross saving once gross investment and acquisition less disposal of nonproduced nonfiancial assets have been deducted. Its value can viewed as the amount available to lend to other units if saving exceeds investment or the amount the corporation is required to borrow to finance investment that cannot be funded from CFC and undistributed profits.

Gross saving, which appears on the right side of the account, consists of both undistributed corporate profits, which have been carried over from the income and outlay account, and CFC. Gross investment, which appears on the left side of the account, consists of both purchases of fixed assets and changes in inventories. Although the structure of the capital account is relatively straightforward, a few additional points should be made about the measures that are shown in this account and their relation to the Federal Reserve Board flow of funds accounts (FFAs).

Net Capital Transfers

Net capital transfers are cash or in-kind transactions that are related to the acquisition or disposal of fixed assets where one of the parties involved in the exchange gets nothing in return. In this account, they consist of investment grants received from the Federal Government.

Gross Investment

This measure differs from the measure of purchases of fixed assets in two ways. First, gross investment does not include purchases of land, which are treated as an acquisition of a nonproduced nonfinancial asset (discussed below). Second, since the national accounts treat software expenditures as investment, gross investment includes expenditures related to the purchase or "in-house" development of software used in production.[27]

Acquisition Less Disposal of Nonproduced Nonfinancial Assets

Nonproduced nonfinancial assets consist of nonfinancial assets that are necessary for production but have not themselves been produced. These assets primarily consist of natural resources, such as land, electromagnetic spectrum, and offshore drilling rights.

Relation to the FFAs

Although the measure of net lending or borrowing that is presented in this account is calculated as the residual claim on gross saving once gross investment and acquisition less disposal of non- produced nonfinancial assets have been deducted, its value can also be calculated by subtracting the acquisition of financial liabilities from the acquisition of financial assets. This alternative calculation works because saving that is not spent on purchases of fixed assets results in the acquisition of financial assets, and borrowing that is used to finance the purchase of fixed assets results in the acquisition of financial liabilities.

The measure of net lending or borrowing links the NIPAs to the FFAs. In particular, the economic accounts that underlie the FFAs begin by subtracting the acquisition of financial liabilities from the acquisition of financial assets to arrive at a measure of net lending or borrowing, which in principle should equal the measure that is calculated in the NIPAs. In practice, these measures differ because they are calculated from different source data and reflect differences in methodologies. The remaining economic accounts then record changes in the value of financial assets and liabilities to finally arrive at a measure for the change in net wealth.[28] As a result, the NIPAs and the FFAs jointly show how the changes in net wealth between balance sheets are related to income from production, much like what is done in financial statements.[29]

III. Economic Accounts for Sectors

This section presents a detailed discussion of the economic accounts for each of the three sectors that contribute to domestic output in the economy—business, households and institutions, and general government. The economic accounts for each sector consist of an aggregation of the individual economic accounts for all related institutions. However, two specific types of manipulations are involved in the aggregation of the accounts for each sector. First, the details provided on the individual accounts are expanded to separately identify the transactions that are made with the other sectors of the economy and the rest of the world. Second, a few types of accounting entries are offset against one another to avoid double counting in important measures presented in the accounts.

Business Sector

The NIPA business sector consists of all entities that produce goods and services for sale at a price intended at least to approximate the costs of production, corporate and noncorporate private enterprises organized for profit, and certain other types of entities. These other types include mutual financial institutions, private noninsured pension funds, cooperatives, nonprofit organizations (that is, entities classified as such by the Internal Revenue Service in determining income tax liability) that primarily serve business, Federal Reserve Banks, federally sponsored credit agencies, and government enterprises.

Since the primary role of business in the economy is to employ resources in the production of final goods and services, most domestic output is produced within this sector.

The structure of the accounts for the business sector is similar to the economic accounts for an individual business firm. However, one notable exception is that the enterprise income and the income and outlay accounts for individual businesses are combined into a single account for the business sector by including measures of taxes on corporate income, of dividend payments, and of undistributed corporate profits as components of the measure of corporate profits on the left side of the account (second panel of table 6). In addition, many of the measures in the accounts for the business sector require further explanation.

Subsidies

This measure, which appears on the left side of the production account, consists of monetary grants from government to private business or to government enterprises at a different level of government (as defined below). Since subsidies are equivalent to negative taxes on production and imports, they are netted against these taxes on the left side of the production account in the calculation of net operating surplus.

Table 6. Economic Accounts for Business

Production Account	
Uses	Sources
Compensation of employees	Gross output
Wages and salaries	Sales
Supplements to wages and salaries	Changes in inventories
Taxes on production and imports	*Less:* Intermediate goods and services
Less: Subsidies	
Consumption of fixed capital	
Net operating surplus	
Private enterprises	
Current surplus of government enterprises	
Charges against gross value added and net operating surplus	Gross value added
Business Enterprise Income Account	
Income payments on assets	Net operating surplus
Production Account	
Uses	Sources
Interest and miscellaneous payments	Income receipts on assets
Dividend payments to the rest of the world	Interest
Reinvested earnings on foreign direct investment in the United States	Dividends received from the rest of the world
Current transfer payments	Reinvested earnings on U.S. direct investment abroad
To persons	
To government	
To the rest of the world	
Current surplus of government enterprises	
Proprietors' income with inventory valuation and capital consumption adjustments	
Rental income of other private business with capital consumption adjustment	
Corporate profits with inventory valuation and capital consumption adjustments	
Less: Taxes on corporate income	
To government	
To the rest of the world	
Equals: Profits after tax	

Net dividends	
Undistributed corporate profits with inventory valuation and capital consumption adjustments	
Uses of enterprise income	Sources of income
Capital Account	
Changes in assets	Sources
Gross investment	Gross saving
Acquisition less disposal of non-produced nonfinancial assets	Undistributed corporate profits with inventory valuation and capital consumption adjustments
Net lending or net borrowing	valuation and capital consumption Consumption of fixed capital Net capital transfers
Gross investment, net acquisition less disposal of nonproduced nonfinancial assets, and net lending	Gross saving and net capital transfers

Net Operating Surplus of Private Enterprises

This measure includes the operating surplus of both incorporated and unincorporated businesses. For corporations, net operating surplus is generally thought to reflect the net return to assets used in production. However, for some unincorporated businesses, net operating surplus may also reflect the value of uncompensated labor contributed by owners. Because this measure reflects a mixture of returns to capital and labor, the SNA refers to this balance as "mixed income" in the case of unincorporated household enterprises. However, the NIPAs use the term operating surplus for all types of business.

Current Surplus of Government Enterprises

The current surplus of government enterprises consists of the net earnings of government agencies that cover a substantial portion of their operating costs by selling goods and services to the public and that maintain their own separate accounts. Typical examples of government enterprises include the U.S. Postal Service, state and local utility companies, and state and local transit authorities. Although many state universities and public parks maintain separate financial records, they are not treated as government enterprises in the accounts because their admissions charges and fees usually cover only a small portion of their operating expenses. Rather, such institutions are treated as part of general government.

The treatment of the current surplus of government enterprises in the accounts is similar to that of net operating surplus of private corporations. In particular, the current surplus is included on the left side of the production account. The only difference in treatment is that the entire value of the current surplus is distributed to the general government. In other words, general government, as the ultimate owner of government enterprises, is assumed to have access to the resources derived from the current surplus of, and to be responsible for investment in, those enterprises.

Reinvested Earnings on Direct Investment

Two additional measures that relate to net income receipts from the rest of the world appear in the income and outlay account for business. The first, reinvested earnings on U.S. direct investment abroad, consists of U.S. investors' claims on current-period undistributed earnings of foreign businesses in which they own or control 10 percent or more of the business. This measure is included as part of income receipts on assets on the right side of the account. The second, reinvested earnings on foreign direct investment in the United States, consists of the foreign investors' claims on the current-period undistributed earnings of domestic U.S. businesses in which they own or control 10 percent or more of the business. This measure is included as part of the income payments on assets on the left side of the account. These flows are included in the account to attribute the earnings of foreign direct investment enterprises to the country of the controlling parent enterprise, regardless of whether the earnings are actually distributed to the parent or are retained and reinvested by the subsidiary.

Proprietors' Income

This measure consists of the net earnings of sole proprietorships, partnerships, and tax-exempt cooperatives that are based on the inventory valuation and depreciation concepts that are used in national economic accounting.[30] Sole proprietorships are businesses that are owned and managed by single individuals who are personally liable for all business debts. For tax purposes, the owners and their businesses are treated as single tax entities. Partnerships are businesses that are owned and managed by two or more persons where at least one person is personally liable for all business debts.[31] For tax purposes, the net earnings of partnerships are "passed through" to owners who report and pay taxes on this income in their personal income tax returns.

The treatment of proprietors' income in the accounts is similar to the treatment of corporate profits. In particular, proprietors' income is included on the left side of the business enterprise income account. Although sole proprietors and partnerships may retain net earnings for future use or investment, a simple accounting convention is used to record the distribution of their income, because of data limitations. In particular, proprietors' income is treated as being distributed entirely to owners in the household and institutions sector, which is consistent with the tax treatment of such income. This treatment is similar to the way the current surplus of government enterprises is attributed to their owners in the government sector.

Rental Income of Other Private Business

This measure consists of the income earned from the rental of properties by landlords who are not sole proprietors or associated with a partnership or corporation and of the royalties received by persons from patents, copyrights, and rights to natural resources. It excludes the rental income of owner-occupants, which is discussed in the section on households and institutions. As with proprietors' income, the rental income of other private business is calculated by using the depreciation concept that is used in national accounting. For tax purposes, the rental income of persons is reported on Schedule E of an individual income tax return. For the economic accounts of the business sector, this income is treated in the same manner as proprietors' income.

Net Dividends

Dividend payments and receipts between domestic businesses are offset against one another to avoid the double counting of corporate profits in the NIPAs. As a result, the measure of net dividends that appears at the bottom of the business enterprise income account consists of dividend payments made by corporations located in the United States and abroad to stockholders who are U.S. residents less the dividend payments received by U.S. corporations.

HOUSEHOLDS AND INSTITUTIONS SECTOR

The NIPA households and institutions sector consists of households and nonprofit institutions serving households (NPISHs). The activities of these two different types of entities are combined into a single sector in the NIPAs because NPISHs provide services to households and because data on nonprofits institutions have traditionally been weak.[32]

As the primary role of households and institutions serving households in the economy is to earn income for consumption or saving by providing resources for production, most of the income that is generated in production is distributed to this sector. Most sales of final goods and services are also made to this sector.

Although the structure of the accounts for households and institutions is similar to that for businesses, there are enough differences to warrant a separate discussion for each of the new accounts.

Production Account

The production account for households and institutions records the value of three different types of output: The rental services provided to homeowners by owner-occupied housing, compensation paid to domestic workers, and nonprofit services that are provided to households. The rest of this section discusses the accounting conventions that are used to record the value of each type of output and the effects that these conventions have on the measure of net operating surplus.

Owner-Occupied Housing Services

As the rental of tenant-occupied housing is counted as a sale of a service and is part of the business sector's output, the services provided by owner-occupied housing must also be counted in GDP. Otherwise, the value of GDP would change every time a housing unit switched between tenant occupied and owner occupied. To avoid this problem an imputation is included in the production account to treat owner-occupied housing in the same manner as rental property in the NIPAs. Although this is done by simply treating homeowners as if they were landlords that rented their own homes to themselves, the actual conventions that are used to record the value of owner-occupied housing are intricate.

On the right side of the account, a measure for space rent is included in the measure of gross output (first panel of table 7). As there are well-developed rental markets for housing, the imputation for space rent is based on the rents that are charged by landlords for equivalent types of property. Spending by homeowners on closing costs, repairs, and property insurance is included in the measure of intermediate goods and services, which is subtracted from gross output to arrive at gross value added, as is done with the similar business expenses for owners of rental property.

On the left side of the account, property taxes paid by homeowners are included in the measure of taxes on production and imports. The measures for subsidies and consumption of fixed capital also include the relevant values for owner-occupied housing. The account is kept in balance by the measure of net operating surplus, which is used for mortgage interest payments and to generate rental income for owner-occupied housing.

Domestic Services

The value of compensation that is paid for domestic services is included in the measures of gross output and gross value added on the right side of the account. This value is also included in the measure of compensation on the left side of the account.

Nonprofit Services

Since nonprofit institutions serving households (NPISHs) often rely on contributions, government grants, and income receipts on assets to cover many of their expenses, sales are not a good measure of the value of their gross output. As a result, the NIPAs value their gross output by the expenses that they incur in production.

On the right side of the account, the value of gross output is calculated as the sum of the compensation of employees, intermediate goods and services, taxes on production and imports (less subsidies), CFC, and mortgage interest. The measure of intermediate goods and services, which is subtracted from gross output to arrive at gross value added, also includes the relevant values for NPISHs.

On the left side of the account, the measures for compensation of employees, taxes on production and imports (less subsidies), CFC, and net interest include the relevant values for NPISHs. These last three types of expenses make up the rental value of fixed assets that are owned and used by NPISHs.

Enterprise Income Account

The enterprise income account for households and institutions shares the same structure as the corresponding account for the business firm, but the account for households and institutions is limited to transactions associated with owner-occupied housing and nonresidential assets owned by NPISHs (second panel of table 7).

Income and Outlay Account

The income and outlay account for households and institutions resembles the corresponding account for business. However, the sources and uses of income that are recorded in the two related accounts differ substantially. Whereas the primary sources of income for business are sales revenues, the primary sources of income for households and institutions are income receipts that are associated with the provision of resources for production (third panel of table 7). The primary use of income for households and institutions is personal consumption expenditures, which has no counterpart for business.

Table 7. Economic Accounts for Households and Institutions

Production Account	
Uses	Sources
Compensation of employees, paid	Gross output 1
Wages and salaries	*Less:* Intermediate goods and services 2
Supplements to wages and salaries	
Taxes on production and imports	
Less: Subsidies	
Consumption of fixed capital	
Net operating surplus	
Charges against gross value added and net operating surplus	Gross value added
Enterprise Income Account	
Interest and miscellaneous payments	Net operating surplus
Current transfer payments	Interest receipts
Rental income of households and institutions with capital consumption adjustment	
Interest payments, transfer payments, and rental income of persons	Sources of income
Income and Outlay Account	
Personal current taxes	Compensation of employees, received
Personal outlays	Wages and salaries
Personal consumption expenditures	Domestic
Interest payments	Rest of the world
Current transfer payments	Supplements to wages and salaries
To government	Proprietors' income with inventory valuation and capital consumption adjustments
To the rest of the world	Rental income of households and institutions with capital consumption adjustment
Personal saving	Income receipts on assets
	Interest received
	Dividends received
	Current transfer receipts
	From government
	From business
	Less: Contributions for government social insurance

Current taxes, outlays, and saving	Personal income
Capital Account	
Uses	Sources
Gross investment	Personal saving
Net lending or borrowing	Net capital transfers
	Consumption of fixed capital
Gross investment and net lending	Gross saving

1. Consists of the sum of wages and salaries paid for domestic services, space rent for owner-occupied housing, and expenses of nonprofit institutions serving households for nonprofit services. The expenses of nonprofit institutions consist of compensation of employees, intermediate goods and services, taxes on production and imports (less subsidies), consumption of fixed capital, and mortgage interest.
2. Consists of the spending of homeowners that would be treated as business expenses by owners of rental property, and purchases of intermediate goods and services by nonprofit institutions serving households.

Another difference between the two related accounts involves the particular accounting entries that are offset against one another to avoid double counting. For business, dividend payments and receipts between domestic businesses are offset against one another. For households and institutions, payments of charitable contributions by households are offset against the receipts of such contributions by NPISHs. As a result, such contributions are excluded from the related account, avoiding a source of double counting in personal income.

In addition to the offsetting for charitable contributions, revenues from sales by NPISHs are deducted from the total expenditures of households and institutions in the measure of personal consumption expenditures that appears on the left side of the account. This practice avoids double counting in GDP because the value of such sales are already reflected in the measures of consumption expenditures or are considered intermediate goods and services in the NIPAs.

Two additional points should be mentioned before turning to a more detailed discussion of the measures in the account. First, because of data limitations, most of the transactions in this account are recorded on a cash basis rather than an accrual basis.[33] Second, payments that are made in households' behalf by business and government are included as both a source and a use of income in this account, even though such receipts and payments are usually excluded from household budgets. For instance, employer-paid health insurance premiums are included in supplements to wages and salaries and the medical care that is paid for by employer health plans is included in personal consumption expenditures.[34] Payments made on households' behalf are included on both sides of the account because they represent sources and uses of income.

Compensation of Employees

Although a general definition for compensation of employees was given in the discussion of the economic accounts for a corporation, there are two notable characteristics about the related measure that appears on the right side of the income and outlay account for households and institutions. First, this measure consists of compensation that is received from all sectors within the domestic economy and the rest of the world, including payments from other households and institutions. Second, this measure includes both receipts-in-kind that represent income as well as employer contributions to employee pension and insurance plans and employer contributions for government social insurance.

Proprietors' Income

This measure consists of the net earnings of sole proprietors and partnerships, which is treated in the accounts as being distributed by business to households.

Rental Income of Persons

This measure consists of both the rental income associated with owner-occupied housing and nonresidential fixed assets owned by NPISHs and the rental income of other private business, which is treated as being distributed by businesses to households.

Current Transfer Receipts

Current transfer receipts from government, which are called government social benefits in the NIPAs, primarily consist of payments that are received by households from social insurance funds and government programs. These funds and programs include social security, hospital insurance, unemployment insurance, railroad retirement, workers' compensation, food stamps, medical care, family assistance, and education assistance. Current transfer receipts from business consist of liability payments for personal injury that are received by households, net insurance settlements that are received by households, and charitable contributions that are received by NPISHs.

Contributions for Government Social Insurance

This item consists of payments made by employers, employees, self-employed, and other individuals that participate in government programs. These programs include social security, hospital insurance, supplemental medical insurance, unemployment insurance, railroad retirement, veterans' life insurance, and temporary disability insurance. Although contributions to such programs constitute a use of income, they are deducted from the sources of income on the right side of the account. This practice is followed so that personal income includes only government social benefits received by the sector rather than both benefits and contributions associated with the same programs.

Personal Current Taxes

This item, which appears on the left side of the account, consists of taxes that are paid by households. These include Federal and state income taxes and state and local taxes on property other than homes, motor vehicle license payments, and other personal license payments. State and local property taxes on homes are excluded from this measure because they are treated as taxes on production.

Personal Consumption Expenditures (PCE)

This measure is simply defined as the value of final goods and services that are purchased by persons. However, there are three noteworthy characteristics about this measure. First, purchases of homes by households and of fixed assets by NPISHs are excluded from PCE because they are classified as fixed investment. Second, although some analysts consider consumer durable goods to be investment, the NIPAs included them in PCE.[35] Purchases of consumer durable goods are included in PCE because they are primarily used for nonmarket household production, which is considered outside the scope of GDP and the NIPAs. Third, PCE includes the value of services provided by NPISHs for the benefit of households as a whole. The value of these services is indirectly calculated by subtracting sales from the measure of NPISHs' output for the reasons mentioned above.

Current Transfer Payments

Current transfer payments to general government in this account primarily consist of donations, fees, and fines that are paid by households and NPISHs to Federal, state, and local governments. Current transfer payments to the rest of the world in this account primarily consist of cash and in-kind transfers to foreign residents by households and NPISHs.

Personal Saving

This measure is the difference between current income and current outlays and taxes—that is, personal consumption expenditures, interest payments, current transfer payments, and current taxes. This measure is conceptually equivalent to undistributed corporate profits in the sense that both measures represent current income that is retained for future use or investment.

Since personal saving is the residual claim on current income, its value can be negative over a number of accounting periods. Such an occurrence is perhaps better understood by considering that current income is not the only source of funds that can be used to finance current consumption. In particular, households and institutions can finance current consumption by using savings from previous periods, by selling financial or fixed assets, or by borrowing. Indeed, in the short-run, an individual household's saving is unlikely to be positive when it makes a major purchase, such as an automobile; even at the aggregate level, personal saving may become negative when an unusually large number of households and institutions make such purchases.

As often noted, personal saving, along with personal income, exclude capital gains. Nevertheless personal saving is still a useful measure for examining the funds that are made available by households and institutions to finance new investment. This is because capital gains represent changes in the value of existing assets and are not a source of new funds for the economy as a whole.

Despite its usefulness, the NIPA measure of personal saving may not be the appropriate measure for some types of analyses that focus on households and institutions. For example, analyses that examine whether households are saving enough for retirement may be better off focusing on households stocks of net wealth, which can be used to finance future consumption.[36]

Capital Account

The structure of the capital account for households and institutions is almost identical to that for the business sector. Investment in this sector consists of the purchase of housing. Net capital transfers in this sector are equal to transfer receipts, which consist of assets that are brought into the United States by immigrants, less transfer payments, which consist of assets removed from the United States by emigrants and of estate taxes that are paid to general government.

General Government Sector

The NIPA general government sector consists of all Federal Government and state and local government agencies except government enterprises.

Governments play many roles in the economy, and the NIPAs provide measures related to at least four of these roles. These include providing nonmarket services for consumption by the general public, investing in assets to provide infrastructure for the economy, providing social benefits to individuals in society, and contributing to domestic saving and investment.

Many of the measures that appear in the general government accounts have already been addressed in the previous sections. For instance, the measure of personal current taxes that appears as a source of income for general government is the same as the measure of personal income taxes that appear as a use of income for households and institutions.[37] The structure of the accounts for the general government sector also resembles that for households and institutions. However, there is no enterprise income account for government enterprises, because of limitations in source data. There are also enough differences between the remaining accounts to warrant a separate discussion for each new account.

Production Account

Because governments primarily rely on tax receipts and transfer payments to cover their expenditures, sales are not a good measure of the value of their gross output. As a result, gross output for general government is measured by the expenditures that are made to provide goods and services for public consumption, but it excludes expenditures for other purposes—for example, social benefits paid to persons, interest payments, and subsidies.

Gross output for general government, which appears on the right side of the account, is calculated as the sum of compensation of employees, purchases of intermediate goods and services, and CFC (as a partial measure of the services of government capital; first panel of table 8). Since purchases of intermediate goods and services are subtracted from gross output to arrive at gross value added, the account is kept in balance by including compensation of employees and CFC on the left side of the account.

BEA recognizes that the inclusion of a measure of net operating surplus in the production account for general government would improve consistency within a full set of national accounts; this practice would also involve choosing a model and using independent source data to estimate the value of a net return to fixed assets. Since the advisory group that has been tasked to recommend updates to the SNA has called for research on to how to measure such a net return in a set of national economic accounts, the production account for this sector presently only includes a measure of CFC, which is an incomplete measure of the cost of capital services derived from such goods.

Table 8. Economic Accounts for General Government

Production Account	
Uses	Sources
Compensation of employees, paid	Gross output 1
Wages and salaries	*Less:* Intermediate goods and services
Supplements to wages and salaries	
Consumption of fixed capital	
Charges against gross value added	Gross value added
Income and Outlay Account	
Uses	Sources
Consumption expenditures	Current tax receipts
Current transfer payments	Personal current taxes
Government social benefits	Taxes on production and imports
To persons	Taxes on corporate income
To the rest of the world	Taxes from the rest of the world
Other current transfer payments to the rest of the world	Contributions for government social insurance Income receipts on assets
Interest payments	Interest and miscellaneous receipts
Subsidies	Dividends
Less: Wage accruals less disbursements	Current transfer receipts
Government saving	From business (net)
	From persons
	Current surplus of government enterprises
Current expenditures and net saving	Current receipts
Capital Account	
Uses	Sources
Gross investment	Government saving
Acquisition less disposal of non-produced nonfinancial assets	Net capital transfers
Net lending or borrowing	Consumption of fixed capital
Gross investment and net lending	Gross saving

Income and Outlay Account

The income and outlay account for general government resembles the corresponding account for households and institutions. However, the nature of income receipts and expenditures that are recorded in the two accounts differ. Whereas the primary sources of income for households and institutions are income receipts from providing resources for production, the primary sources of income for the general government are current tax receipts and contributions for government social insurance (second panel of table 8). General government also does not use income receipts mainly for financing consumption expenditures. Rather, much of the income received by general government is also used to provide current transfer payments to households.

Another difference between the two accounts involves the particular accounting entries that are offset against one another to avoid double counting. For households, payments and receipts of charitable contributions between households and institutions are offset against one another. For general government, income payments and receipts between the Federal Government and the state and local governments, which are called grants-in-aid in the NIPAs, are offset against one another. As a result, grants-in-aid are excluded from the measures of the consolidated government account, though they are included in the separate ac- counts for the Federal Government and for state and local governments. This practice avoids a potential source of double counting in the measures of government receipts and expenditures.

In addition to the offsetting of grants-in-aid, revenue from sales to other sectors is deducted from the total expenditures of general government in the formation of the measure of government consumption expenditures. As with the offsetting of the sales of NPISHs against the expenditures of households and institution expenditures, this practice avoids double counting in GDP because such sales are already reflected in the measures of PCE and exports or are considered purchases of intermediate goods and services by business.

Government Consumption Expenditures

This item, which appears on the right side of the account, provides a measure of the value of services produced by government for the benefit of society as a whole. Examples of such services include national defense, public education, and police and fire protection. The value of government consumption expenditures is indirectly calculated by subtracting own-account investment, which is counted as part of government gross investment, and sales to other sectors from the measure of government gross output for the reason mentioned above.

Wage Accruals Less Disbursements

This item consists of wages and salaries earned less wages and salaries paid. It is subtracted from expenditures on the left side of account so that the measure of net government saving on an accounting basis is comparable to that of personal saving. This can be understood by noting that the wages and salaries in government consumption expenditures are on an accrual basis..

Net Government Saving

This item is the residual claim on government current receipts once current expenditures have been deducted. This measure reflects, among other factors, the transactions that are covered (for example, transactions of government employee retirement plans) and the time at which transactions are recorded that make it different from measures of surpluses or deficits that are included in government budgets.[38]

Capital Account

The structure of the capital account for general government is almost identical to that for households and institutions. In fact, the only structural difference is that the account for the general government includes a measure for the net acquisition of nonproduced nonfinancial assets from the business sector.

Although the structure of the related accounts is similar to those of the business sector, the measure of gross investment differs because it excludes changes in inventories. Although their inclusion would improve overall consistency in the NIPAs, a complete set of data that could be used to construct such a related measure is not available.

IV. NIPA Summary Accounts

This section provides the conceptual framework for the NIPA summary accounts:

- The domestic income and product account
- The private enterprise income account
- The personal income and outlay account
- The government receipts and expenditures account
- The foreign transactions current account
- The domestic capital account
- The foreign transactions capital account

Since the personal income and outlay account and the government receipts and expenditure account are identical to the related income and outlay accounts that were presented for each of the related sectors in the last section, only the remaining accounts need further discussion.

Domestic Income and Product Account

This account mainly consists of an aggregation of the underlying production accounts for all domestic sectors. However, a major difference between the related accounts is that the right side of the domestic income and product account measures GDP by using the expenditure approach rather than the value-added approach (first panel of table 9). This means that GDP is calculated in the NIPAs as the sum of PCE, gross private domestic investment, net exports of goods and services, and government consumption expenditures and gross investment. Longtime users of the accounts are familiar with this derivation of GDP.

Although measures of gross output, intermediate goods and services, and gross value added by sector are not presented in the domestic income and product account, measures of gross value added by sector can be found in NIPA table 1.3.5. In addition, measures of gross output, intermediate goods and services, and gross value added by industry can be found in the BEA's industry accounts.

GDI, which appears on the left side of the account, includes a measure of wage and salary accruals. However, the account also provides measures for wage and salary disbursements and for wage accruals less disbursements to identify counter-entries in the complete set of summary accounts.

Although most of the measures that appear in the domestic income and product account have already been introduced, a few of the new measures should be explained.

Gross Private Domestic Investment

This item, which appears on the right side of the account, consists of the sum of gross private fixed investment and change in private inventories. Gross private fixed investment consists of purchases of fixed assets by businesses and NPISHs and of the construction of new housing for households.

Net Exports of Goods and Services

This measure is defined as exports less imports. Exports are added on the right side of the account because they are part of the value of final goods and services produced in the United States that are not included in the other measures of final expenditures in the account. Imports, which include purchases of both final and intermediate goods and services, are subtracted on the right side of the account because they are produced outside of the United States but are included in the other measures of final expenditures.

Statistical Discrepancy

Although the value of GDI should equal the value of GDP, in practice, the values of these measures often differ. This is because each is calculated using a different set of methodologies and data sources. The statistical discrepancy that appears on the left side of the account shows how much the two measures differ.

BEA views GDP as a more reliable measure of output than GDI because it considers the source data underlying GDP to be more timely and accurate. For instance, most of the annual source data used for estimating GDP are based on complete enumerations, such as Federal Government budget data, or are regularly adjusted to such enumerations, such as the quinquennial economic and government censuses. GDP is also based largely on the detailed benchmark input-output accounts that are available every five years. For GDI, only the annual tabulations of employment tax returns and Federal Government budget data are based on complete enumerations, and only farm proprietors' income and state and local government budget data are adjusted to complete enumeration. Most of the remaining components of GDI are calculated using tabulations of samples of tax returns, which become available for a given year with a more considerable lag than much of the data that is used to estimate GDP.[39]

Private Enterprise Income Account

There are two main differences between the private enterprise income account and the business enterprise income account that was presented in the last section. First, the private enterprise income account consists of an aggregation of the private income accounts for both the business and the households and institutions sectors (second panel of table 9). Second, the private enterprise income account excludes interest and transfer transactions and the surplus associated with government enterprises, which are shown in the government receipts and expenditures account.

As noted earlier, the right side of the private enterprise income account shows the sources of income as the net operating surplus and income receipts of businesses on assets (such as financial assets and equity in other businesses). The left side of the account shows the uses of income as income payments on assets (such as holders of financial liabilities and equity claims of other businesses), business current transfer payments, and income that accrues to the owners of business (namely proprietors' income, rental income of persons, and corporate profits). Corporate profits, a widely used measure in the United States, is distributed to government (taxes on corporate income) and to shareholders (net dividends), or is retained by the corporations (undistributed corporate profits).

Foreign Transactions Current Account

This account shows the current payments received from the United States by the rest of the world and the current receipts received by the United States from the rest of the world. The balance on this account is equal to U.S. exports of goods and services and income receipts from the rest of the world less U.S. imports of goods and services, income payments to the rest of the world, and current tax and net current transfer payments made to the rest of the world. This balance is closely related to the current account in the international transactions accounts. The current account balance can be viewed as the acquisition of foreign assets by U.S. residents less the acquisition of U.S. assets by foreign residents.

Domestic Capital Account

This account consists of an aggregation of the capital accounts for each sector that contributes to domestic output, where net saving is equal to the sum of personal saving, undistributed corporate profits, wage accruals less disbursements, and net government saving. However, there are two notable differences between this account and those presented for each individual sector.

The first difference is that the domestic capital account combines the measures of net capital transfers and of acquisitions and disposals of nonproduced nonfinancial assets into a single measure of "capital account transactions" on the left side of the account (sixth panel of table 9). This practice simplifies the structure of the domestic capital account and the system of counter-entries in the summary accounts.

The second difference is that the domestic capital account includes the statistical discrepancy on the right side of the account. The measures of saving that are carried forward into this account are ultimately based on measures of income that is generated from production. By including the statistical discrepancy, the measure of saving at the bottom of the account becomes more consistent with the measure of the value of final goods and services that BEA believes is more accurate.

Foreign Transactions Capital Account

This account subtracts net capital transactions with the rest of the world from the balance on the foreign transactions current account to derive the net lending or borrowing position that the United States has with the rest of the world. The measures of net capital transactions and of net lending or borrowing in this account are identical to those included in the domestic capital account.

Table 9. Summary National Income and Product Accounts, 2006
[Billions of dollars]
Account 1. Domestic Income and Product Account

Line		
1	Compensation of employees, paid	7,454.8
2	Wage and salary accruals.	6,032.2
3	Disbursements (3–12 and 5–11).	6,024.7
4	Wage accruals less disbursements (4–9 and 6–11)	7.5
5	Supplements to wages and salaries (3–14)	1,422.6
6	Taxes on production and imports (4–16)	967.3
7	*Less:* Subsidies (4–8)	49.7
8	Net operating surplus.	3,225.3
9	Private enterprises (2–19).	3,239.2
10	Current surplus of government enterprises (4–26)	–13.9
11	Consumption of fixed capital (6–13)	1,615.2
12	Gross domestic income	13,212.8
13	Statistical discrepancy (6–19)	–18.1
14	GROSS DOMESTIC PRODUCT	13,194.7
15	Personal consumption expenditures (3–3)	9,224.5
16	Durable goods ..	1,048.9
17	Nondurable goods	2,688.0
18	Services	5,487.6
19	Gross private domestic investment...	2,209.2
20	Fixed investment (6–2) .	2,162.5
21	Nonresidential.	1,397.7
22	Structures .	405.1
23	Equipment and software..	992.6
24	Residential..	764.8
25	Change in private inventories (6–4)	46.7
26	Net exports of goods and services	–762.0
27	Exports (5–1).	1,467.6
28	Imports (5–9)	2,229.6
29	Government consumption expenditures and gross	2,523.0

	investment (4–1 and 6–3)	
30	Federal	932.5
31	National defense.	624.3
32	Nondefense .	308.2
33	State and local.	1,590.5
34	GROSS DOMESTIC PRODUCT ..	13,194.7

Account 2. Private Enterprise Income Account

Line		
1	Income payments on assets.	3,109.3
2	Interest and miscellaneous payments (3–20 and 4–21)	2,946.8
3	Dividend payments to the rest of the world (5–14)	91.4
4	Reinvested earnings on foreign direct investment in the United States (5–15)	71.1
5	Business current transfer payments (net)	90.2
6	To persons (net) (3–24)	27.2
7	To government (net) (4–24).	60.6
8	To the rest of the world (net) (5–19)	2.5
9	Proprietors' income with inventory valuation and capital consumption adjustments (3–17)	1,006.7
10	Rental income of persons with capital consumption adjustment (3–18)	54.5
11	Corporate profits with inventory valuation and capital consumption adjustments	1,553.7
12	Taxes on corporate income	453.9
13	To government (4–17)....	435.5
14	To the rest of the world (5–19)	18.4
15	Profits after tax with inventory valuation and capital consumption adjustments	1,099.8
16	Net dividends (3–21 and 4–22) .	698.9
17	Undistributed corporate profits with inventory valuation and capital consumption adjustments (6–10	400.9
18	USES OF PRIVATE ENTERPRISE INCOME	5,814.5
19	Net operating surplus (1–9)	3,239.2
20	Income receipts on assets..	2,575.3
Line		
21	Interest (3–20)	2,155.5
22	Dividend receipts from the rest of the world (5–6).	167.2
23	Reinvested earnings on U.S. direct investment abroad (5–7).	252.6
24	SOURCES OF PRIVATE ENTERPRISE INCOME	5,814.5

Account 3. Personal Income and Outlay Account

Line		
1	Personal current taxes (4–15)	1,354.3
2	Personal outlays	9,590.3
3	Personal consumption expenditures (1–15)	9,224.5
4	Personal interest payments (3–20) .	238.0
5	Personal current transfer payments .	127.8
6	To government (4–25) .	78.9
7	To the rest of the world (net) (5–17)	48.9
8	Personal saving (6–9)	38.8
9	PERSONAL TAXES, OUTLAYS, AND SAVING.	10,983.4
10	Compensation of employees, received	7,440.8
11	Wage and salary disbursements	6,018.2
12	Domestic (1–3 less 5–11)	6,015.3
13	Rest of the world (5–3)	2.9
14	Supplements to wages and salaries (1–5) .	1,422.6
15	Employer contributions for employee pension and insurance funds	970.7
16	Employer contributions for government social insurance	451.8
17	Proprietors' income with inventory valuation and capital consumption adjustments (2–9).	1,006.7
18	Rental income of persons with capital consumption adjustment (2–10)..	54.5
19	Personal income receipts on assets	1,796.5
20	Personal interest income (2–2 and 3–4 and 4–7 and 5–5 less 2–21 less 4–21 less 5–13)	1,100.2
21	Personal dividend income (2–16 less 4–22)..	696.3
22	Personal current transfer receipts	1,612.5
23	Government social benefits (4–4).	1,585.3
24	From business (net) (2–6)...	27.2
25	*Less:* Contributions for government social insurance (4–19).	927.6
26	PERSONAL INCOME .	10,983.4

Account 4. Government Receipts and Expenditures Account

Line		
1	Consumption expenditures (1–29)	2,089.3
2	Current transfer payments..	1,618.3
3	Government social benefits	1,588.7
4	To persons (3–23)	1,585.3
5	To the rest of the world (5–18) .	3.3
6	Other current transfer payments to the rest of the world (net) (5–18)	29.6
7	Interest payments (3–20)	372.9
8	Subsidies (1–7)	49.7
9	*Less:* Wage accruals less disbursements (1–4).	0.0
10	Net government saving (6–12).	–195.4
11	Federal	–220.0
12	State and local	24.6
13	GOVERNMENT CURRENT EXPENDITURES AND NET SAVING.	3,934.8
14	Current tax receipts .	2,769.8
15	Personal current taxes (3–1) .	1,354.3
16	Taxes on production and imports (1–6) .	967.3
17	Taxes on corporate income (2–13)	435.5
18	Taxes from the rest of the world (5–18)	12.6
19	Contributions for government social insurance (3–25)	927.6
20	Income receipts on assets...	111.9
21	Interest and miscellaneous receipts (2–2 and 3–20)..	109.3
22	Dividends (3–21) .	2.6
23	Current transfer receipts	139.5
24	From business (net) (2–7)	60.6
25	From persons (3–6) .	78.9
26	Current surplus of government enterprises (1–10)	–13.9
27	GOVERNMENT CURRENT RECEIPTS	3,934.8

Account 5. Foreign Transactions Current Account

Line		
1	Exports of goods and services (1–27)	1,467.6
2	Income receipts from the rest of the world.	691.4
3	Wage and salary receipts (3–13) .	2.9
4	Income receipts on assets .	688.6
5	Interest (3–20)	268.8
Line		
6	Dividends (2–22).	167.2
7	Reinvested earnings on U.S. direct investment abroad (2–23) .	252.6
8	CURRENT RECEIPTS FROM THE REST OF THE WORLD	2,159.0
9	Imports of goods and services (1–28) .	2,229.6
10	Income payments to the rest of the world.	633.4
11	Wage and salary payments (1–3).	9.4
12	Income payments on assets	624.0
13	Interest (3–20) .	461.5
14	Dividends (2–3)	91.4
15	Reinvested earnings on foreign direct investment in the United States (2–4)	71.1
16	Current taxes and transfer payments to the rest of the world (net).	90.1
17	From persons (net) (3–7).	48.9
18	From government (net) (4–5 and 4–6 less 4–18)	20.3
19	From business (net) (2–8 and 2–14) ...	20.9
20	Balance on current account, national income and product accounts (7–1).	–794.1
21	CURRENT PAYMENTS TO THE REST OF THE WORLD AND BALANCE ON CURRENT ACCOUNT	2,159.0

Account 6. Domestic Capital Account

Line		
1	Gross domestic investment..	2,642.9
2	Private fixed investment (1–20)	2,162.5
3	Government fixed investment (1–29)	433.8
4	Change in private inventories (1–25)	46.7
5	Capital account transactions (net) (7–2) .	3.9
6	Net lending or net borrowing (–), national income and product accounts (7–3).	–798.0
7	GROSS DOMESTIC INVESTMENT, CAPITAL ACCOUNT TRANSACTIONS, AND NET LENDING	1,848.8
8	Net saving.	251.7
9	Personal saving (3–8).	38.8
10	Undistributed corporate profits with inventory valuation and capital consumption adjustments (2–17)	400.9
11	Wage accruals less disbursements (private) (1–4) .	7.5
12	Net government saving (4–10) .	–195.4
13	*Plus:* Consumption of fixed capital (1–11)	1,615.2
14	Private	1,347.5
15	Government.	267.7
16	General government	223.6
17	Government enterprises.	44.1
18	*Equals:* Gross saving...	1,866.9
19	Statistical discrepancy (1–13)	–18.1
20	GROSS SAVING AND STATISTICAL DISCREPANCY.	1,848.8

Account 7. Foreign Transactions Capital Account

Line		
1	BALANCE ON CURRENT ACCOUNT, NATIONAL INCOME AND PRODUCT ACCOUNTS (5–20)	–794.1
2	Capital account transactions (net) (6–5).	3.9
3	Net lending or net borrowing (–), national income and product accounts (6–6)	–798.0
4	CAPITAL ACCOUNT TRANSACTIONS (NET) AND NET LENDING, NATIONAL INCOME AND PRODUCT ACCOUNTS	–794.1

REFERENCES

[1] See "GDP: One of the Great Inventions of the 20th Century," SURVEY OF CURRENT BUSINESS 80 (January 2000): 6–14.
[2] New users of the NIPAs may find it beneficial to first review "Measuring the Economy: A Primer on GDP and the National Income and Product Accounts" on <www.bea.gov>.
[3] Information on the data and estimating methods underlying the NIPAs is available in component methodologies available on BEA's Web site at <www.bea.gov>.
[4] See U.S. Bureau of Economic Analysis, "Concepts and Methods of the U.S. Input-Output Accounts," September 2006, at <www.bea.gov/bea/ mp.htm>; and see Brian C. Moyer, Mark A. Planting, Mahnaz Fahim Nader, and Sherlene K.S. Lum, "Preview of the Comprehensive Revision of the Annual Industry Accounts: Integrating the Annual Input-Output Accounts and the Gross-Domestic-Product-by-Industry Accounts, SURVEY 84 (March 2004): 38–51.
[5] See U.S. Board of Governors of the Federal Reserve System, *Guide to the Flow of Funds Accounts,* Board of Governors, Washington, D.C., 2006; and see Albert M. Teplin, "The U.S. Flow of Funds Accounts and Their Uses," *Federal Reserve Bulletin* (July 2001): 431–441.
[6] See Commission of the European Communities, International Monetary Fund, Organization for Economic Co-operation and Development, United Nations, and the World Bank, *System of National Accounts 1993* (Brussels/Luxembourg, New York, Paris, and Washington, DC, 1993). For more on the SNA and the relationship between it and the NIPAs, see Charles Ian Mead, Karin E. Moses, and Brent R. Moulton, "The NIPAs and the System of National Accounts," SURVEY 84 (December 2004): 17–32.
[7] *SNA 1993*: paragraph 6.15. 8.
[8] *SNA 1993*, paragraph 6.22.
[9] See Brent R. Moulton, Robert P. Parker, and Eugene P. Seskin, "Preview of the 1999 Comprehensive Revision of the National Income and Product Accounts: Definitional and Classificational Changes," SURVEY 79 (August 1999): 8–11.
[10] The SNA's definition of an imputation is restricted to estimates of goods and services for which there is no observable exchange. Estimates for which there is an observable exchange but no observable price are referred to simply as estimates. See paragraphs 1.72–1.75 and 3.34 of the SNA.
[11] The imputations in the NIPAs are presented in NIPA table 7.12.

[12] In the I-O accounts, "all industries" includes government industries (such as the U. S. Postal Service) and certain "special industries" (such as owner-occupied housing).

[13] However, in BEA's international transactions accounts, Puerto Rico, the U.S. territories, and the Northern Mariana Islands are treated as part of the United States. See NIPA table 4.3B, "Relation of Foreign Transactions in the National Income and Product Accounts to the Corresponding Items in the International Transactions Accounts."

[14] "U.S. residents" includes individuals, governments, business enterprises, trusts, associations, nonprofit organizations, and similar institutions that have the center of their economic interest in the United States and that reside or expect to reside in the United States for 1 year or more. (For example, business enterprises residing in the United States include U.S. affiliates of foreign companies.) In addition, U.S. residents include all U.S. citizens who reside outside the United States for less than 1 year and U.S. citizens residing abroad for 1 year or more who meet one of the following criteria: Owners or employees of U.S. business enterprises who reside abroad to further the enterprises' business and who intend to return within a reasonable period; U.S. Government civilian and military employees and members of their immediate families; and students who attend foreign educational institutions.

[15] Households are treated as businesses for the purpose of recording the ownership of and investment in housing.

[16] BEA prepares separate accounts for fixed assets and consumer durables, available at <www.bea.gov>. In these accounts, purchases of consumer durables are treated as investment in assets, and these assets depreciate over time. BEA's use of the term "capital" in reference to this stock of fixed assets is different from the conventional use of the term to refer to financial holdings.

[17] Many of the formal accounting practices used in financial accounting, such as double-entry bookkeeping, can be traced all the way back to merchants and bankers in Florence, Venice, and Genoa during the thirteenth and fifteenth centuries. In contrast, the formal accounting framework for national accounting was introduced by Richard Stone in 1940 (See Angus Deaton, "Stone, Richard John Nicholas" in J. Eatwell, M. Milgate and P. Newman, eds., *The New Palgrave: A Dictionary of Economics,* Macmillian: London, 1987, vol. 4: 509–512).

[18] A fully articulated set of national accounts actually leads to a quadruple-entry system. However, transactions are usually recorded only twice in the

national income and product accounts (NIPAs) because the changes in assets or liabilities that are associated with the changes in the revenues and expenses are recorded in the Federal Reserve Board flow of funds accounts.

[19] Additional detail on financial accounting practices can be found in many of the standard textbooks on the subject, such as John J. Wild, *Financial Accounting: Information for Decisions* (McGraw-Hill College, 2006) and as Jerry J. Weygandt, Donald K. Kieso, and Paul D. Kimmel, *Financial Accounting: Tools for Decision Making, with Annual Report* (John Wiley & Sons Inc., 2003).

[20] The period of time that is used to define current assets is either the period of a year or an operating cycle, whichever is longer. An operating cycle is the average period of time between the initial purchase of intermediate goods and services and the collection of accounts receivable for the related sales of products.

[21] An accurate determination of the costs that can be directly linked to the production of goods and services is one of the more difficult tasks in financial accounting. As a result, many corporations simply rely on fixed ratios to allocate a certain percentage of expenses to this category.

[22] Business firms may also calculate net cash flows from operating activities using a more direct method that lists major classes of gross receipts and gross expenditures. However, the indirect method presented in this paper is more commonly used.

[23] More specifically, only changes in inventories of work in progress and finished goods are added to sales in the derivation of gross output. Changes in materials and supplies inventories are deducted from purchases of intermediate goods and services to derive intermediate consumption. This practice is consistent with showing consumption of materials and supplies when used in production rather than when purchased. Although only work-in-progress and finished goods inventories are added to sales in calculating gross output, all three types of inventories are included in the measure of "changes in private inventories" that is used to calculate GDP in the expenditure approach of calculating GDP

[24] For additional information on the calculation of CFC, see the chapter entitled "Concepts and Methods" in Bureau of Economic Analysis, *Fixed Assets and Consumer Durable Goods in the United States, 1925–97* (Washington, DC: U.S. Government Printing Office, September 2003).

[25] For a discussion of the treatment of the transactions associated with commercial banks and with property and casualty insurance companies, see Brent R. Moulton and Eugene P. Seskin, "Preview of the 2003 Compre-

hensive Revision of the National Income and Product Accounts," SURVEY 83 (June 2003): 17–34.

[26] Since the more detailed tables of the NIPAs also provide measures of corporate profits that are based on data reported to the Internal Revenue Service, the adjustments that are applied in the derivation of the measures in this account are explicitly mentioned in the title for this measure.

[27] For a discussion of the treatment of software investment in the NIPAs, see Brent R. Moulton, Robert P. Parker, and Eugene P. Seskin, "A Preview of the 1999 Comprehensive Revision of the National Income and Product Accounts: Definitional and Classification Changes," SURV E Y 79 (August 1999): 7–20.

[28] Because of data limitations, the set of balance sheets provided in the FFAs do not cover all sectors in the economy.

[29] BEA and the Federal Reserve Board have been working together to further integrate the NIPAs and the FFAs. One outcome of these efforts is the development of a set of integrated accounts that use consistent terminology for a consistently defined set of sectors. For more on this topic see, Charlotte Anne Bond, Teran Martin, Susan Hume McIntosh, and Charles Ian Mead, "Integrated Macroeconomic Accounts for the United States," SURV E Y 87 (February 2007): 14–31.

[30] Since the more detailed tables of the NIPAs also provide measures of proprietors' income that are based on data reported to the Internal Revenue Service, the adjustments that are applied in the derivation of the measures in this account are explicitly mentioned in the title for this measure.

[31] The term "persons" in this context is defined by the Uniform Partnership Act and covers a broad set of legal entities, including individuals, business trusts, estates, and trusts.

[32] By combining the activities of households and of nonprofit institutions serving households into a single consolidated account, transactions between these separate types of entities did not need to be presented. However, due to increased data availability in more recent years, information on the incomes and outlays for each of these types of entities is available in NIPA table 2.9. For a discussion of NIPA table 2.9, see Charles Ian Mead, Clinton P. McCully, and Marshall B. Reinsdorf, "Income and Outlays of Households and of Nonprofit Institutions Serving Households," SURVEY 83 (April 2003): 13–17

[33] Most business transactions, such as interest payments and receipts, are likely to be recorded on an accrual basis.

[34] For further examples of payments made in households' behalf, see the BEA methodology paper *Personal Consumption Expenditures* at <www.bea.gov/bea/mp.htm>.

[35] In the NIPAs, consumer durable goods are defined as tangible commodities that have an average life of three or more years. Although consumer durable goods are treated as consumption in the NIPAs, the value of the stock of such goods is included in the BEA's tables of fixed assets and consumer durable goods. In addition, the value of the stock of consumer durable goods is included in the net worth measures that are maintained in the Federal Reserve Board's FFAs.

[36] For a further discussion of usefulness of personal saving in particular types of analyses, see Marshall B. Reinsdorf, "Alternative Measures of Personal Savings," SURVEY 87 (February 2007): 7–13.

[37] Since each measure in the summary accounts of the NIPAs has a counter-entry, additional examples of such relationships can be found in table 9.

[38] For a more detailed discussion of the relationship between the Federal deficits or surpluses and NIPA net saving, see Mary L. Roy and Andrew P. Cairns, "Federal Budget Estimates for Fiscal Year 2009," SURVEY 87 (March 2007): 10–21.

[39] For a further discussion of the statistical discrepancy, see Robert B. Parker and Eugene P. Seskin, "Annual Revision of the National Income and Product Accounts," SURVEY 77 (August, 1997): 6–35.

In: Measuring the Economy: GDP and NIPAs ISBN: 978-1-60741-199-4
Editor: Kemal Sahin © 2009 Nova Science Publishers, Inc.

Chapter 3

A GUIDE TO THE NATIONAL INCOME AND PRODUCT ACCOUNTS OF THE UNITED STATES*

Bureau of Economic Analysis

This guide presents information on the structure, definitions, and presentation that underlie the national income and product accounts (NIPAs) produced by the Bureau of Economic Analysis. The NIPAs show the composition of production and the distribution of incomes earned in production. Thus, they represent a critical element of the U.S. economic accounts, which are designed to provide a consistent and comprehensive picture of the Nation's economy. The NIPAs feature several widely followed measures of aggregate U.S. economic activity, including gross domestic product (GDP), gross domestic income (GDI), personal income, and personal saving among others. This guide is organized as follows:

BACKGROUND AND HISTORY OF THE NIPAS

The estimation of national income was initiated during the early 1930s, when the lack of comprehensive economic data frustrated the efforts of Presidents Hoover and Roosevelt to design policies to combat the Great Depression. In response to this need, the Department of Commerce commissioned Simon

* This is an edited, excerpted and augmented edition of a Bureau of Economic Analysis publication

Kuznets of the National Bureau of Economic Research (NBER) to develop estimates of national income. Professor Kuznets headed a small group within the Bureau of Foreign and Domestic Commerce's Division of Economic Research. Professor Kuznets coordinated the work of researchers at the NBER in New York and his staff at Commerce. The estimates were presented in a report to the Senate in 1934, *National Income, 1929–32*.

The entry of the United States into World War II led to increased demand for data that could be used for wartime planning. Early in 1942, annual estimates of gross national product (GNP) were introduced to complement the estimates of national income. In addition, estimates were developed to detail how income was generated, received, and spent by various sectors of the economy.

The U.S. national income and product statistics were first presented as part of a complete and consistent accounting system in the July 1947 supplement to the SURVEY OF CURRENT BUSINESS. The supplement contained 48 tables covering the years 1929–46. All estimates were presented in current dollars; no adjustments were yet made for changes in purchasing power. Quarterly estimates were available for only a few of the aggregates (national income, GNP, and personal income, and their major components). Monthly estimates were presented for personal income and its major components.

In 1951, annual estimates of real GNP and of implicit price deflators were introduced as supplementary tables. Real GNP was calculated by holding fixed the prices of a particular base year that is—GNP was calculated in "constant dollars." In 1954, these inflation- adjusted estimates were formally integrated into the standard NIPA tables.

Another revision, published in 1958, introduced changes in the accounting system and added new information to the accounts. Five summary accounts were adopted as a concise, general presentation of output, income, outlays, foreign transactions, saving, and investment. Quarterly estimates of real GNP were introduced. Government sector tables provided a new breakdown of expenditures by type and function for the Federal Government and for state and local governments. The foreign transactions tables were expanded in detail and integrated with the balance of payments accounts. Regional estimates were introduced, as were estimates of the net stock of fixed assets in manufacturing.

In the 1965 comprehensive revision, for the first time, the components of GNP were benchmarked to the detailed estimates contained in the 1958 input-output table, which provided a better understanding of the structural relationships within the economy.

During the 1960s and 1970s, the estimates of capital stock were expanded to cover all business and government owned fixed assets and consumer durable goods. In 1976, in order to provide a more consistent valuation, the estimates of consumption of fixed capital (CFC) were shifted to a current-cost basis. Previously, the estimates were on a book-value basis—that is, valued at historical cost—reflecting a mixture of prices for the various years in which the assets were acquired.

In 1985, BEA introduced quality-adjusted price indexes for computers and peripheral equipment that were developed with the assistance and advice of researchers from the IBM Corporation. The indexes, which were based on a statistical technique known as "hedonic" regression, adjusted for the rapid improvements in speed and capacity of computer equipment. These hedonic price indexes provide improved measures of price change for computers and peripheral equipment during periods when quality characteristics change rapidly and when prices decline as new products are introduced.

In 1991, BEA changed its featured measure of U.S. production from GNP to GDP. GDP covers the goods and services produced by labor and property located in the United States and is thus consistent with key economic indicators of employment, productivity, and industry output. The change also facilitated comparisons of economic activity in the United States with that in other countries.

In 1993, the *System of National Accounts 1993 (SNA 1993)* was adopted by the international community in order to facilitate international comparisons of national economic statistics and to serve as a guide for countries as they develop their economic accounting systems.[1] BEA actively participated in preparing *SNA 1993* and announced its plan to move toward consistency with *SNA 1993*. Since then, the major improvements in the NIPAs have been designed, at least in part, to incorporate the SNA's concepts and definitions wherever feasible.[2]

In 1996, BEA introduced several major improvements to the NIPAs. BEA began estimating the changes in real GDP and its components by chaining together year-by-year quantity changes that were calculated using the Fisher index formula, rather than estimating real GDP on the basis of prices of a single, arbitrary base year.[3] Government expenditures for equipment and structures were recognized as fixed investment, thereby providing a more complete measure of investment through the consistent treatment of fixed assets whether purchased by the public or the private sector. The method for calculating CFC was changed to reflect the results of studies on the prices of used equipment and structures in resale markets that found that depreciation generally tends to follow a geometric pattern.

The 1999 comprehensive revision of the NIPAs further improved the definitions underlying the accounts and the statistical underpinnings of the current-dollar estimates, quantities, and prices in the accounts. For example, business and government expenditures for software were recognized as fixed investment. Government employee retirement plans were reclassified so that they would be treated similarly to private pension plans. A new method was introduced for calculating the real value of unpriced bank services by incorporating measures of banking activity. The consumer price indexes that were used for deflating personal consumption expenditures (PCE) were revised back to 1978 to reflect the use of a geometric mean formula.

The most recent comprehensive revision of the NIPAs, which was released beginning in 2003, further improved and updated the accounts. For example, a more complete and accurate measure of insurance services was adopted that includes estimates of the implicit services provided by property and casualty insurance companies; the new measure eliminates large swings in measured insurance services associated with catastrophic losses. An improved measure of banking services that includes the services received by borrowers was introduced; previously, such services were only allocated to depositors. A new treatment of government activity that recognizes that governments produce services and that goods and services purchased by governments are intermediate inputs was adopted. An expanded definition of national income that includes all net incomes earned in production was introduced; the new definition is more consistent with international guidelines. The presentation of the NIPAs was changed to reflect these improvements and to introduce a redesigned set of tables that provides more information in an easier to use format and that offers more flexibility for the addition of new tables. The new tables also improve the comparability of the NIPAs with other U.S. accounts (such as the Federal Reserve Board's flow of funds accounts) and with accounts of other nations and the System of National Accounts.

The improvements introduced over the years have reflected not only BEA's own experience, research, and strategic planning but also the reviews and recommendations of scholars and other experts.

In the 1950s, there were two major reviews of the accounts. The first was prepared by the NBER.[4] The second resulted from a symposium on the accounts held by the Conference on Research in Income and Wealth.[5] Both of these reviews dealt with emerging issues of the time, many of which related to expanding the complexity and scope of the accounts to more accurately portray the U.S. economy. They also dealt with conceptual issues, such as the treatment of capital gains and the coverage of nonmarket production and consumption, and they discussed the need for better integration of the income and product accounts, flow of funds, and other aspects of the existing accounts.

In 1971, on the occasion of the 50th anniversary of the SURVEY, BEA published a special volume containing 43 papers contributed by some of the country's most prominent economists.[6] BEA catalogued and prioritized the suggestions from these papers, and BEA's Director at that time, George Jaszi, responded to them.

In 1977, a report was prepared by the Advisory Committee on Gross National Product Data Improvement (referred to as the Creamer Report after its chair, Daniel Creamer).[7] The report addressed concerns about the relatively large revisions to the GNP estimates in the early 1970s and focused on needed improvements in the source data.

In 1979, the Conference on Research in Income and Wealth addressed several aspects of the NIPAs role as a system of information about the behavior of the economy.[8] Topics included the concepts and structure of the accounts, deflation and the treatment of quality change in price indexes, and source data. The last topic included an evaluation of major parts of the Creamer Report.

In 1982, the General Accounting Office published a report that reviewed quarterly GNP revisions in order to reevaluate the relative importance of the Creamer Report's recommendations and to reassess the reliability of the GNP estimates.[9] The report focused more on statistical than on conceptual issues and suggested that priorities be placed on those recommendations that would most reduce GNP revisions. In addition, as the title indicates, it urged BEA to take a more proactive role in obtaining the source data needed to improve the accounts.

In 1995, BEA began a comprehensive review of its national, international, and regional economic accounts. Outside perspective was obtained by comments and discussions of a strategic plan that BEA presented in the SURVEY and at a conference of users.[10]

In 2000, BEA established an advisory committee that meets about twice a year to discuss issues and possible improvements to the accounts. The papers that are presented to the advisory committee are made available on BEA's Web site <www.bea.gov>.

In 2004, BEA participated in a Conference on Research in Income and Wealth on "A New Architecture for the U.S. National Accounts."[11] The purpose of the conference was to initiate the development of a comprehensive and fully integrated set of U.S. national accounts. Conference participants identified short-term and long-term initiatives to more fully integrate the existing sets of accounts, to uncover gaps and inconsistencies, and to expand and integrate systems of non- market accounts with the core system. As part of this exercise, participants identified initiatives to integrate BEA's existing set of accounts with other U.S. economic accounts, including the productivity accounts prepared by the Bureau of Labor Statistics and the flow of funds accounts prepared by the Federal Reserve Board.

DEFINITIONS AND CLASSIFICATIONS UNDERLYING THE NIPAS

NIPA Entries

The national income and product accounts (NIPAs) are summarized in seven accounts that show the composition of production and the distribution of incomes earned in production.[12] The seven summary accounts are shown in table A. For illustrative purposes, the tables show estimates for 2005 that are based on the latest published NIPA estimates.

Each of the components in the summary accounts also enters one of the other summary accounts and is shown in one or more of the tables that make up the full set of 299 NIPA tables. Taken together, the summary accounts constitute a double-entry system in which a use (or expenditure) recorded in one account for one sector is also recorded as a source (or receipt) in an account of another sector or of the same sector.[13] This system of integrated, double-entry accounts provides a comprehensive measure of economic activity in a consistently defined framework without double counting. Thus, the NIPAs, in combination with BEA's industry, wealth, and regional accounts, can be used to trace the principal economic flows among the major sectors of the economy.

The first account, the domestic income and product account, shows the consolidated—that is, unduplicated—production of all sectors of the economy as the sum of goods and services sold to final users on the right side and the income generated by that production on the left side.[14] The private enterprise income account (account 2) provides additional information on the sources and uses of income by private enterprises, which give rise to the bulk of the output in the U.S. economy. Accounts 3–5 show the receipts and expenditures of the other major sectors of the U.S. economy: The personal sector, which is made up of households and nonprofit institutions serving households; the government sector; and the foreign sector. Account 6 provides information on the saving and investment of the domestic sectors of the economy, and account 7 provides information on capital transactions with the rest of the world.

Within the summary accounts, each entry has a counterentry, generally in another account. The parenthetical numbers that follow an entry in table A identify the counterentry by account and line number. With the exception of major income and product aggregates, entries are usually defined in the sequence in which they appear in the seven-account summary. The definition is not repeated where the counterentry appears, but a cross reference is made to the place of its first appearance. After the seven-account-summary discussion, definitions for the following items are presented: Final sales of domestic product, gross domestic purchases, final sales to domestic purchasers, net interest, fixed assets, produced assets, nonproduced assets, population, personal saving as a percentage of disposable personal income, gross saving as a percentage of gross national income, U.S. residents, foreign residents, and the rest of the world.

Major Aggregates

Gross domestic product (GDP) (1–34), the featured measure of U.S. output, is the market value of the goods and services produced by *labor and property located in the United States*.[15] Because the labor and property are located in the United States, the suppliers— that is, the workers and, for property, the owners— may be either U.S. residents or residents of the rest of the world.

Gross domestic income (GDI) (1–12) measures output as the costs incurred and the incomes earned in the production of GDP.[16] In theory, GDP should equal GDI, but in practice, they differ because their components are estimated using largely independent and less than perfect source data. This difference is termed the "statistical discrepancy" (described below).

Gross national product (GNP) is the market value of the goods and services *produced by labor and property supplied by U.S. residents*. Because the labor and property are supplied by U.S. residents, they may be located either in the United States or abroad. The difference between GDP and GNP is net receipts of income from the rest of the world. These net receipts represent income from the goods and services produced abroad using labor and property supplied by U.S. residents less payments to the rest of the world for the goods and services produced in the United States using labor and property supplied by foreign residents. The income receipts and payments are measured as compensation of employees, corporate profits (earnings of both incorporated and unincorporated affiliates), and interest.

Net domestic product (NDP) is the net market value of the goods and services attributable to labor and property located in the United States and is equal to GDP less consumption of fixed capital (CFC). NDP may be viewed as an estimate of sustainable product, which is a rough measure of the level of consumption that can be maintained while leaving capital assets intact.

Net national product (NNP) is the net market value of goods and services attributable to the labor and property supplied by U.S. residents and is equal to GNP less CFC. The measure of CFC used for both NDP and NNP relates only to fixed capital located in the United States. The investment in capital is measured by private fixed investment and government gross investment.

National income includes all net incomes (net of CFC) earned in production.[17] National income is the sum of compensation of employees, proprietors' income with inventory valuation adjustment (IVA) and capital consumption adjustment (CCAdj), rental income of persons with CCAdj, corporate profits with IVA and CCAdj, net interest and miscellaneous payments, taxes on production and imports, business current transfer payments, and the current surplus of government enterprises, less subsidies.[18]

Gross national income (GNI) is equal to national income plus CFC. (GNI and GNP also differ by the statistical discrepancy.)

Personal income (3–26) is the income received by persons from all sources—that is, from participation in production and from current transfer receipts from both government and business. "Persons" consists of individuals, nonprofit institutions that primarily serve households, private noninsured welfare funds, and private trust funds. Personal income is calculated as compensation of employees, received; proprietors' income with IVA and CCAdj; rental income of persons with CCAdj; personal income receipts on assets; and personal current transfer receipts; less contributions for government social insurance.

Disposable personal income is personal income less personal current taxes. It is the income available to persons for spending or saving.

Account 1. Domestic Income and Product Account

This account presents the product and the income produced by labor and property located in the United States.

Table A. Summary National Income and Product Accounts, 2005
[Billions of dollars]
Account 1. Domestic Income and Product Account

Line		
1	Compensation of employees, paid	7,036.6
2	Wage and salary accruals	5,671.1
3	Disbursements (3–12 and 5–11).	5,671.1
4	Wage accruals less disbursements (4–9	0.0
5	Supplements to wages and salaries (3–14)	1,365.5
6	Taxes on production and imports (4–16)	922.4
7	*Less:* Subsidies (4–8)	57.3
8	Net operating surplus	2,878.2
9	Private enterprises (2–19)	2,893.6
10	Current surplus of government enterprises	–15.4
11	Consumption of fixed capital (6–13).	1,604.8
12	Gross domestic income	12,384.8
13	Statistical discrepancy (6–19)	71.0
14	GROSS DOMESTIC PRODUCT	12,455.8
15	Personal consumption expenditures (3–3)	8,742.4
16	Durable goods	1,033.1
17	Nondurable goods .	2,539.3
18	Services.	5,170.0
19	Gross private domestic investment.	2,057.4
20	Fixed investment (6–2)	2,036.2
21	Nonresidential.	1,265.7
22	Structures .	338.6
23	Equipment and software.	927.1
24	Residential..	770.4
25	Change in private inventories (6–4).	21.3
26	Net exports of goods and services	–716.7
27	Exports (5–1).	1,303.1
28	Imports (5–9)	2,019.9
29	Government consumption expenditures and gross investment (4–1 and 6–3).	2,372.8
30	Federal.	878.3
31	National defense.	589.3
32	Nondefense .	289.0
33	State and local.	1,494.4
34	GROSS DOMESTIC PRODUCT	12,455.8

Account 2. Private Enterprise Income Account

Line		
1	Income payments on assets.	2,552.4
2	Interest and miscellaneous payments (3–20 and 4–21)	2,411.4
3	Dividend payments to the rest of the world (5–14).	81.8
4	Reinvested earnings on foreign direct investment in the United States (5–15)	59.2
5	Business current transfer payments (net)	74.2
6	To persons (net) (3–24) .	45.7
7	To government (net) (4–24).	30.1
8	To the rest of the world (net) (5–19)	–1.6
9	Proprietors' income with inventory valuation and capital consumption	970.7
10	adjustments (3–17)	72.8
11	Rental income of persons with capital consumption adjustment (3–18)	1,330.7
12	Corporate profits with inventory valuation and capital consumption adjustments ..	399.3
13	Taxes on corporate income	384.4
14	To government (4–17)	14.9
15	To the rest of the world (5–19)	931.4
16	Profits after tax with inventory valuation and capital consumption adjustments.	576.9
17	Net dividends (3–21 and 4–22)	354.5
18	Undistributed corporate profits with inventory valuation and capital	5,000.7
Line		
19	Net operating surplus (1–9)	2,893.6
20	Income receipts on assets..	2,107.1
21	Interest (3–20)	1,769.1
22	Dividend receipts from the rest of the world (5–6).	320.0
23	Reinvested earnings on U.S. direct investment abroad (5–7).	18.0
24	SOURCES OF PRIVATE ENTERPRISE INCOME.	5,000.7

Account 3. Personal Income and Outlay Account

Line		
1	Personal current taxes (4–15)	1,203.1
2	Personal outlays	9,070.9
3	Personal consumption expenditures (1–15)	8,742.4
4	Personal interest payments (3–20)	209.4
5	Personal current transfer payments .	119.2
6	To government (4–25)	72.0
7	To the rest of the world (net) (5–17)	47.1
8	Personal saving (6–9)	–34.8
9	PERSONAL TAXES, OUTLAYS, AND SAVING..	10,239.2
10	Compensation of employees, received	7,030.3
11	Wage and salary disbursements	5,664.8
12	Domestic (1–3 less 5–11).	5,661.9
13	Rest of the world (5–3)	2.9
14	Supplements to wages and salaries (1–5)	1,365.5
15	Employer contributions for employee pension and insurance funds	933.2
16	Employer contributions for government social insurance	432.3
17	Proprietors' income with inventory valuation and capital consumption adjustments (2–9)	970.7
18	Rental income of persons with capital consumption adjustment (2–10).	72.8
19	Personal income receipts on assets .	1,519.4
20	Personal interest income (2–2 and 3–4 and 4–7 and 5–5 less 2–21 less 4–21 less 5–13)	945.0
21	Personal dividend income (2–16 less 4–22).	574.4
22	Personal current transfer receipts .	1,526.6
23	Government social benefits (4–4)	1,480.9
24	From business (net) (2–6)	45.7
25	*Less:* Contributions for government social insurance (4–19)	880.6
26	PERSONAL INCOME	10,239.2

Account 4. Government Receipts and Expenditures Account

Line		
1	Consumption expenditures (1–29)	1,975.7
2	Current transfer payments	1,517.8
3	Government social benefits	1,484.0
4	To persons (3–23).	1,480.9
5	To the rest of the world (5–18) .	3.1
6	Other current transfer payments to the rest of the world (net) (5–18).	33.9
7	Interest payments (3–20)	348.0
8	Subsidies (1–7) .	57.3
9	*Less:* Wage accruals less disbursements (1–4).	0.0
10	Net government saving (6–12).	–312.5
11	Federal	–309.2
12	State and local	–3.3
13	GOVERNMENT CURRENT EXPENDITURES AND NET SAVING	3,586.3
14	Current tax receipts .	2,520.7
15	Personal current taxes (3–1).	1,203.1
16	Taxes on production and imports (1–6)	922.4
17	Taxes on corporate income (2–13)	384.4
18	Taxes from the rest of the world (5–18)	10.8
19	Contributions for government social insurance (3–25)	880.6
20	Income receipts on assets..	98.3
21	Interest and miscellaneous receipts (2–2 and 3–20)	95.8
22	Dividends (3–21)	2.4
23	Current transfer receipts	102.1
24	From business (net) (2–7)	30.1
25	From persons (3–6)	72.0
26	Current surplus of government enterprises (1–10)	–15.4
27	GOVERNMENT CURRENT RECEIPTS .	3,586.3

GDP is measured as the sum of personal consumption expenditures, gross private domestic investment (including change in private inventories and before deduction of charges for CFC), net exports of goods and services (exports less imports), and government consumption expenditures and gross investment. GDP excludes intermediate purchases of goods and services by business.

Account 5. Foreign Transactions Current Account

Line		
1	Exports of goods and services (1–27)	1,303.1
2	Income receipts from the rest of the world	513.3
3	Wage and salary receipts (3–13)	2.9
4	Income receipts on assets	510.4
5	Interest (3–20).	172.4
6	Dividends (2–22)	320.0
7	Reinvested earnings on U.S. direct investment abroad (2–23)	18.0
8	CURRENT RECEIPTS FROM THE REST OF THE WORLD	1,816.5
9	Imports of goods and services (1–28) .	2,019.9
10	Income payments to the rest of the world.	481.5
11	Wage and salary payments (1–3).	9.2
12	Income payments on assets	472.2
13	Interest (3–20)	331.2
14	Dividends (2–3)	81.8
15	Reinvested earnings on foreign direct investment in the United States (2–4)	59.2
16	Current taxes and transfer payments to the rest of the world (net).	86.6
17	From persons (net) (3–7)..	47.1
18	From government (net) (4–5 and 4–6 less 4–18) .	26.1
19	From business (net) (2–8 and 2–14)	13.3
20	Balance on current account, national income and product accounts (7–1)	–771.4
21	CURRENT PAYMENTS TO THE REST OF THE WORLD AND BALANCE ON	1,816.5

Personal consumption expenditures (PCE) (1–15) measures goods and services purchased by U.S. residents. PCE consists mainly of purchases of new goods and of services by individuals from private business. In addition, PCE includes purchases of new goods and of services by nonprofit institutions (including compensation of employees), net purchases of used goods by individuals and nonprofit institutions, and purchases abroad of goods and services by U.S. residents. PCE also includes purchases of certain goods and services provided by general government and government enterprises, such as tuition payments for higher education, charges for medical care, and charges for water and other sanitary services. Finally, PCE includes imputed purchases that keep PCE invariant to changes in the way that certain activities are carried out—for example, whether housing is rented or owned, whether financial services are explicitly charged, or whether employees are paid in cash or in kind.

Account 6. Domestic Capital Account

Line		
1	Gross domestic investment.	2,454.5
2	Private fixed investment (1–20)	2,036.2
3	Government fixed investment (1–29)	397.1
4	Change in private inventories (1–25) .	21.3
5	Capital account transactions (net) (7–2)	4.4
6	Net lending or net borrowing (–), national income and product accounts (7–3)	–775.8
7	GROSS DOMESTIC INVESTMENT, CAPITAL ACCOUNT TRANSACTIONS, AND NET LENDING	1,683.1
8	Net saving.	7.2
9	Personal saving (3–8).	–34.8
10	Undistributed corporate profits with inventory valuation and capital consumption adjustments (2–17)	354.5
11	Wage accruals less disbursements (private) (1–4) .	0.0
12	Net government saving (4–10)	–312.5
13	*Plus:* Consumption of fixed capital (1–11)	1,604.8
14	Private .	1,352.6
15	Government.	252.2
16	General government.	207.2
17	Government enterprises..	45.1
18	*Equals:* Gross saving.	1,612.0
19	Statistical discrepancy (1–13)	71.0
20	GROSS SAVING AND STATISTICAL DISCREPANCY.	1,683.1

The following conventions are used to classify each PCE commodity: Durable goods (1–16) are tangible commodities that can be stored or inventoried and that have an average life of at least 3 years; nondurable goods (1–17) are all other tangible commodities that can be stored or inventoried; and services (1–18) are commodities that cannot be stored and that are consumed at the place and time of purchase.

Account 7. Foreign Transactions Capital Account

Line		
1	BALANCE ON CURRENT ACCOUNT, NATIONAL INCOME AND PRODUCT ACCOUNTS (5–20)	–771.4
2	Capital account transactions (net) (6–5)	4.4
3	Net lending or net borrowing (–), national income and product accounts (6–6)	–775.8
4	CAPITAL ACCOUNT TRANSACTIONS (NET) AND NET LENDING, NATIONAL INCOME AND PRODUCT ACCOUNTS	–771.4

Note: Numbers in parentheses indicate accounts and items of counterentry in the accounts. For example, line 5 of account 1 is shown as "Supplements to wages and salaries (3–14)"; the counterentry is shown in account 3, line 14.

Gross private domestic investment (1–19) consists of fixed investment (1–20) and the change in private inventories (1–25). Fixed investment consists of both nonresidential (1–21) fixed investment and residential (1–24) fixed investment. It is measured without a deduction for CFC and includes replacements and additions to the capital stock. It covers all investment in fixed assets by private businesses and by nonprofit institutions in the U.S., regardless of whether the fixed asset is owned by U.S. residents. (Purchases of the same types of equipment, software, and structures by government agencies are included in government gross investment.) It excludes investment by U.S. residents in other countries. Nonresidential fixed investment consists of both structures (1–22) and equipment and software (1–23).

Nonresidential structures consists of new construction (including own-account production), improvements to existing structures, expenditures on new nonresidential mobile structures, brokers' commissions on sales of structures, and net purchases of used structures by private business and by nonprofit institu tions from government agencies.[19] New nonresidential construction includes hotels and motels and mining exploration, shafts, and wells. Nonresidential structures also includes equipment considered to be an integral part of a structure, such as plumbing, heating, and electrical systems.

Equipment and software consists of purchases by private business and by nonprofit institutions of new machinery, equipment, furniture, vehicles, and computer software used repeatedly, or continuously, in the processes of production for more than 1 year. Also included are dealers' margins on sales of used equipment to business and to nonprofit institutions; net purchases of used equipment from government agencies, from persons, and from the rest of the world; and own-account production of computer software. For equipment that is purchased for both business and personal use (for example, motor vehicles), the personal-use portion is included in PCE.

Residential fixed investment consists of all private residential structures and of residential equipment that is owned by landlords and rented to tenants. Residential structures consists of new construction of permanent-site single family and multifamily units, improvements (additions, alterations, and major structural replacements) to housing units, expenditures on manufactured homes, brokers' commissions on the sale of residential property, and net purchases of used structures from government agencies. Residential structures includes some types of equipment that are built into the structure, such as heating and air conditioning equipment.

Change in private inventories (1–25) is the change in the physical volume of inventories owned by private business, valued in average prices of the period. It differs from the change in the book value of inventories reported by most business; the difference is the inventory valuation adjustment (described above).

Net exports of goods and services (1–26) is exports (1–27) less imports (1–28) of goods and services. Income receipts and payments and current taxes and transfer payments to the rest of the world (net) are excluded.

Government consumption expenditures and gross investment (1–29), the measure of government sector final demand, consists of two major components: Current consumption expenditures by general government and gross investment by both general government and government enterprises. Consumption expenditures consists of the goods and services that are produced by general government, less sales to other sectors and own-account investment. As producers of nonmarket services, governments generally provide services to the general public without charge, for example, law enforcement services, national defense services, and elementary and secondary education. The value of government production, that is, government's gross output, is measured by the cost of inputs: Compensation of employees, CFC (a partial measure of the services of government capital), and intermediate goods and services purchased.[20] Therefore, government consumption expenditures is measured as the sum of these costs of production less sales by government of goods and services to other sectors (which are classified as PCE, if purchased by individuals, or as intermediate inputs, if purchased by businesses) and the value of software and construction that are produced by government for its own use (that is, own-account investment, which is classified as part of gross government investment). Gross investment consists of purchases of new structures and of equipment and software by both general government and government enterprises, net purchases of used structures and equipment, and own-account production of structures and of software. Government consumption expenditures and gross investment does not include current transactions of government enterprises, current transfer payments, interest payments, subsidies, or transactions in financial assets and in nonproduced assets such as land.

Compensation of employees, paid (1–1) shows the income accruing to employees as remuneration for their work for domestic production; it includes compensation paid to the rest of the world and excludes compensation received from the rest of the world. It is the sum of wage and salary accruals and of supplements to wages and salaries.

Wage and salary accruals (1–2) consists of the monetary remuneration of employees, including the compensation of corporate officers; commissions, tips, and bonuses; voluntary employee contributions to certain deferred compensation plans, such as 401(k) plans; employee gains from exercising nonqualified stock options; receipts-in-kind; and miscellaneous compensation of employees.[21] Wage and salary accruals consists of disbursements (1–3) and wage accruals less disbursements (1–4). Disbursements is wages and salaries as just defined except that retroactive wage payments are recorded when paid rather than when earned. Accruals less disbursements is the difference between wages earned, or accrued, and wages paid, or disbursed. In the NIPAs, wages accruals is the measure used for gross domestic income, and wage disbursements is the measure used for personal income.

Supplements to wages and salaries (1–5) consists of employer contributions for employee pension and insurance funds (3–15) and of employer contributions for government social insurance (3–16).

Taxes on production and imports (1–6) consists of Federal excise taxes and custom duties and of state and local sales taxes, property taxes (including residential real estate taxes), motor vehicle licenses, severance taxes, special assessments, and other taxes.

Subsidies (1–7) is the monetary grants paid by government agencies to private business and to government enterprises at another level of government.[22]

Net operating surplus (1–8) is a profits-like measure that shows business income after subtracting the costs of compensation of employees, taxes on production and imports (less subsidies), and CFC from gross product (or value added), but before subtracting financing costs (such as net interest) and business current transfer payments. Net operating surplus consists of net operating surplus of private enterprises (1–9) and current surplus of government enterprises (1–10).

(Net operating surplus of private enterprises is discussed under account 2 below.) The current surplus of government enterprises is their current operating revenue and subsidies received from other levels of government less their current expenses. In the calculation of their current surplus, no deduction is made for net interest paid.

Consumption of fixed capital (CFC) (1–11) is the charge for the using up of private and government fixed capital located in the United States. It is defined as the decline in the value of the stock of fixed assets due to wear and tear, obsolescence, accidental damage, and aging. For most types of assets, estimates of CFC are based on geometric depreciation patterns; empirical studies on the prices of used equipment and structures in resale markets have concluded that a geometric pattern of depreciation is appropriate for most types of assets.[23] For general government and for nonprofit institutions that primarily serve individuals, CFC is recorded in government consumption expenditures and in PCE, respectively, as a partial measure of the value of the current services of the fixed assets owned and used by these entities. Private capital consumption allowances consists of tax return-based depreciation charges for corporations and nonfarm proprietorships and of historical cost depreciation (calculated by BEA using a geometric pattern of price declines) for farm proprietorships, rental income of persons, and nonprofit institutions. Private capital consumption adjustment is the difference between private capital consumption allowances and private CFC.

Statistical discrepancy (1–13) is GDP less GDI or GNP less GNI. It is recorded in the NIPAs as an "income" component that reconciles the income side with the product side of the accounts. As noted above, it arises because the two sides are estimated using independent and imperfect data.[24]

Account 2. Private Enterprise Income Account

This account presents *sources of private enterprise income* (2–24) on the right side of the account and *uses of private enterprise income* (2–18) on the left side.[25] Private enterprises consist of private businesses and the accounts of homeowners for owner-occupied housing (which is treated as if it were a business). In addition, the net interest paid by nonprofit institutions serving households is included as a use of income in this account.[26]

Net operating surplus, private enterprises (2–19), can be derived by a series of deductions from business-sector gross value added, as described above. Alternatively, it can be calculated as the sum of the domestic components of proprietors' income with inventory valuation adjustment (IVA) and capital consumption adjustment (CCAdj), rental income of persons with CCAdj, corporate profits with IVA and CCAdj, net interest and miscellaneous payments, and business current transfer payments (net).[27]

Income receipts on assets (2–20) consists of interest, dividend receipts from the rest of the world, and reinvested earnings on U.S. direct investment abroad. *Interest* (2–21) is the interest received by domestic private enterprises and includes both monetary and imputed interest receipts. Interest received by private noninsured pension plans is recorded as being directly received by persons in personal income. *Dividend receipts from the rest of the world* (2–22) consists of receipts by U.S. residents of dividends from foreign corporations plus earnings distributed by unincorporated foreign affiliates to their U.S. parents. *Reinvested earnings on U.S. direct investment abroad* (2–23) consists of receipts by U.S. residents of their share of the reinvested earnings of their incorporated foreign affiliates and reinvested earnings of their unincorporated foreign affiliates.

The uses of private enterprise income (2–18) consists of income payments on assets, business current transfer payments (net), proprietors' income with IVA and CCAdj, rental income of persons with CCAdj, and corporate profits with IVA and CCAdj.

Income payments on assets (2–1) consists of interest and miscellaneous payments, dividend payments to the rest of the world, and reinvested earnings on foreign direct investment in the United States. *Interest and miscellaneous payments* (2–2) consists of interest paid by domestic private enterprises and of rents and royalties paid by private enterprises to government.[28] Interest payments includes both monetary and imputed interest payments. *Dividend payments to the rest of the world* (2–3) consists of payments by U.S. corporations of dividends to foreign residents, plus earnings distributed by unincorporated U.S. affiliates to their foreign parents. *Reinvested earnings on foreign direct investment in the United States* (2–4) consists of payments to foreign residents of their share of the reinvested earnings of their incorporated U.S. affiliates and reinvested earnings of their unincorporated U.S. affiliates. These earnings are treated as income payments on assets because the decision to retain some of the earnings within a U.S. enterprise represents a deliberate investment decision on the part of the foreign investor.[29]

Business current transfer payments (net) (2–5) consists of payments *to persons (net)* (2–6), *to government (net)* (2–7), and *to the rest of the world (net)* (2–8) by private business for which no current services are performed. Payments for net insurance settlements—actual insured losses (or claims payable) less a normal level of losses—are also treated as business current transfer payments. Business current transfer payments to government (net), consists of Federal deposit insurance premiums and other current transfer payments (largely fines and regulatory and inspection fees), less net insurance settlements from the National Flood Insurance Program, state and local fines and other current transfer payments (largely donations and tobacco settlements), and net insurance settlements paid to state and local governments as policyholders. Business current transfer payments to the rest of the world (net) consists of net insurance settlements paid to the rest of the world as policyholders.

Proprietors' income with inventory valuation and capital consumption adjustments (2–9) is the current- production income (including income in kind) of sole proprietorships and partnerships and of tax-exempt cooperatives. The imputed net rental income of owner occupants of farm and nonfarm dwellings is included in rental income of persons. Proprietors' income excludes dividends and monetary interest received by nonfinancial business and rental income received by persons not primarily engaged in the real estate business; these incomes are included in dividends, net interest, and rental income of persons.

Rental income of persons with capital consumption adjustment (2–10) is the net current production income of persons (except those primarily engaged in the real estate business) from the rental of real property, the imputed net rental income of owner occupants of farm and nonfarm dwellings, and the royalties received by persons from patents, copyrights, and rights to natural resources.

Corporate profits with inventory valuation and capital consumption adjustment (2–11) is the net current production income of organizations treated as corporations in the NIPAs. These organizations consist of all entities required to file Federal corporate tax returns, including mutual financial institutions and cooperatives subject to Federal income tax, private noninsured pension funds, nonprofit institutions that primarily serve business, Federal Reserve banks, and federally sponsored credit agencies.[30] With several differences, this income is measured as receipts less expenses as defined in Federal tax law. Among these differences are the following: Receipts exclude capital gains and dividends received, expenses exclude depletion and capital losses and losses resulting from bad debts, inventory withdrawals are valued at replacement cost, and depreciation is on a consistent accounting basis and is valued at replacement cost using depreciation profiles based on empirical evidence on used asset prices that generally suggest a geometric pattern of price declines. Corporate profits is included on a national income basis, which is defined as the income of U.S. residents; therefore the profits component includes income earned abroad by U.S. corporations and excludes income earned in the United States by the rest of the world.

Taxes on corporate income (2–12) consists of taxes on corporate income paid to government and taxes on corporate income paid to the rest of the world. *Taxes on corporate income paid to government* (2–13) is the sum of Federal, state, and local government income taxes on all income subject to taxes; this income includes capital gains and other income excluded from profits before tax. The taxes are measured on an accrual basis, net of applicable tax credits. *Taxes on corporate income paid to the rest of the world* (2–14) consists of nonresident taxes—that is, taxes paid by domestic corporations to foreign governments.

Profits after tax with inventory valuation adjustment and capital consumption adjustment (2–15) is corporate profits with IVA and CCAdj less taxes on corporate income. It consists of net dividends and undistributed corporate profits with IVA and CCAdj. Net div*idends* (2–16) is payments in cash or other assets, excluding the corporations' own stock, that are made by corporations located in the United States and abroad to stockholders who are U.S. residents. The payments are measured net of dividends received by U.S. corporations. Dividends paid to state and local governments are included. *Undistributed profits with inventory valuation and capital consumption adjustments* (2–17) is corporate profits after tax with IVA and CCAdj less net dividends.

Account 3. Personal Income and Outlay Account

Personal income is the sum of compensation of employees, received; proprietors' income with IVA and CCAdj; rental income of persons with CCAdj; personal income receipts on assets; and personal current transfer receipts; less contributions for government social insurance. Personal income receipts on assets (interest, dividends, and rent) of private noninsured pension plans and of government employee retirement plans are recorded as being received directly by persons in the corresponding components of personal income.

Compensation of employees, received (3–10) consists of wage and salary disbursements and supplements to wages and salaries.

Wage and salary disbursements (3–11) consists of *domestic disbursements* (see 1–3) and *rest-of-the-world disbursements* (3–13).

Supplements to wages and salaries (see 1–5) consists of employer contributions for employee pension and insurance funds and of employer contributions for government social insurance. *Employer contributions for employee pension and insurance funds* (3–15) consists of employer payments (including payments in kind) to private pension and profit-sharing plans, publicly administered government employee retirement plans, private group health and life insurance plans, privately administered workers' compensation plans, and supplemental unemployment benefit plans. *Employer contributions for government social insurance* (3–16) consists of employer payments under the following Federal Government and state and local government programs: Old age, survivors, and disability insurance (social security); hospital insurance; unemployment insurance; railroad retirement; pension benefit guaranty; veterans life insurance; publicly administered workers' compensation; military medical insurance; and temporary disability insurance.[31]

Proprietors' income with inventory valuation and capital consumption adjustments (see 2–9).

Rental income of persons with capital consumption adjustment (see 2–10).

Personal income receipts on assets (3–19) consists of personal interest income and personal dividend income. *Personal interest income* (3–20) is the interest income (monetary and imputed) of persons, including individuals and nonprofit institutions serving households, from all sources. It equals private enterprise interest payments (see 2–2) plus *personal interest payments* (3–4), plus *government interest payments* (4–7), plus *interest receipts from the rest of the world* (5–5), less *private enterprise interest receipts* (see 2–21), less *government interest receipts* (see 4–2 1), less *interest payments to the rest of the world* (5–13). *Personal interest payments* (3–4) consists of all interest paid by individuals except mortgage interest, which is reflected in rental income of persons.

Personal dividend income (3–21) is the dividend income of persons from all sources. It equals *net dividends paid by corporations* (see 2–16) less *government receipts of dividends* (4–22), which consists of dividends received by state and local governments.

Personal current transfer receipts (3–22) consists of income payments to persons for which no current services are performed and of net insurance settlements. It is shown as the sum of government social benefits and current transfer receipts from business (net) (see 2–6). *Government social benefits* (3–23) includes benefits from government social insurance funds and social assistance benefits from certain other programs.

Contributions for government social insurance (3–25) includes employer contributions for government social insurance (see 3–16) and payments by employees, self employed, and other individuals who participate in the following government programs: Old age, survivors, and disability insurance (social security); hospital insurance; supplementary medical insurance, including the Medicare Prescription Drug benefit; unemployment insurance; railroad retirement; veterans life insurance; and temporary disability insurance.

Personal current taxes (3–1) is tax payments (net of refunds) by U.S. residents that are not chargeable to business expense. Personal taxes includes taxes on income, including realized net capital gains, and on personal property. Personal contributions for government social insurance is not included. Taxes paid by U.S. residents to foreign governments and taxes paid by foreigners to the U.S. Government are both included in *current taxes and transfer payments to the rest of the world from government (net).*

Personal outlays (3–2) is the sum of personal consumption expenditures (see 1–15), personal interest payments (see 3–4), and personal current transfer payments. *Personal current transfer payments* (3–5) consists of transfer payments *to government* (3–6) and *to the rest of the world* (3–7). Payments to government includes donations, fees, and fines paid to Federal, state, and local governments. Payments to the rest of the world is personal remittances in cash and in kind to the rest of the world less such remittances from the rest of the world.

Personal saving (3–8) is personal income less the sum of personal outlays and personal current taxes. It is the current saving of individuals (including proprietors and partnerships), nonprofit institutions that primarily serve households, life insurance carriers, private noninsured welfare funds, private noninsured pension plans, publicly administered government employee retirement plans, and private trust funds. Personal saving may also be viewed as the net acquisition of financial assets (such as cash and deposits, securities, and the change in life insurance and pension fund reserves), plus the net investment in produced assets (such as residential housing, less depreciation), less the net increase in financial liabilities (such as mortgage debt, consumer credit, and security credit), less net capital transfers received.

Account 4. Government Receipts and Expenditures Account

Government current receipts (4–27) is the sum of current tax receipts, contributions for government social insurance, income receipts on assets, current transfer receipts, and current surplus of government enterprises. *Current tax receipts* (4–14) consists of personal current taxes (see 3–1), taxes on production and imports (see 1–6), taxes on corporate income (see 2–13), and *taxes from the rest of the world* (4–18), which are mostly income taxes received by the Federal Government from foreigners.[32]

Contributions for government social insurance (see 3–25).

Income receipts on assets (4–20) consists of interest and miscellaneous receipts and dividends. *Interest and miscellaneous receipts* (4–21) includes monetary and imputed interest received by government on loans and investments from persons, from business, and from the rest of the world; miscellaneous receipts include Federal Outer Continental Shelf royalties and state and local rents and royalties. (Interest received by government employee retirement plans is recorded as being received directly by persons in personal income.)

Dividends received by government (see 3–21).

Current transfer receipts (4–23) consists of receipts *from business (net)* (4–24) (see 2–7) and receipts *from persons* (4–25) (see 3–6).

Current surplus of government enterprises (see 1–10). *Consumption expenditures* (see 1–29).

Current transfer payments (4–2) is government so- cial benefits and other current transfer payments to the rest of the world. *Government social benefits* (4–3) consists of government social benefits payments to *persons* (4–4) (see 3–23) and government social benefits payments *to the rest of the world* (4–5), which are U.S. Government transfers, mainly social security benefits, to former residents of the United States. *Other current transfer payments to the rest of the world (net)* (4–6) consists of U.S. Government military and nonmilitary grants in cash and nonmilitary grants-in-kind to foreign governments.

Interest payments (4–7) is interest paid by government to persons, to business, and to the rest of the world (that is, to foreign businesses, governments, and persons). Interest paid consists of monetary interest paid on public debt and other financial obligations.

Subsidies (see 1–7).

Wage accruals less disbursements (see 1–4).

Net government saving (4–10) is the sum of govern- ment current receipts (lines 14, 19, 20, 23, and 26 of account 4) less the sum of government current expenditures (lines 1, 2, 7, 8, less line 9 of account 4). It may also be viewed as the net acquisition of financial assets by government and government enterprises, plus the net investment in fixed assets (such as roads and highways, less depreciation), plus the net government purchases of nonproduced assets, less the net increase in financial liabilities, less net capital transfers.

Account 5. Foreign Transactions Current Account

Imports of goods and services (see 1–28).

Income payments to the rest of the world (5–10) consists of wage and salary payments (see 1–3) and income payments on assets (5–12), which is the sum of interest (see 3–20), dividends (see 2–3), and reinvested earnings on foreign direct investment in the United States (see 2–4).

Current taxes and transfer payments to the rest of the world (net) is the sum of transfer payments *from persons (net)* (see 3–7), *from government (net)* (see 4–5 and 4–6 less 4–18), and *from business (net)* (see 2–8 and 2–14).

Balance on current account, national income and product accounts (5–20) is U.S. exports of goods and services and income receipts from the rest of the world less U.S. imports of goods and services, income payments to the rest of the world, and current taxes and transfer payments to the rest of the world (net). It may also be viewed as the acquisition of foreign assets by U.S. residents less the acquisition of U.S. assets by foreign residents. It includes the statistical discrepancy in the balance of payments accounts.

Exports of goods and services (see 1–27).

Income receipts from the rest of the world (5–2) consists of wage and salary receipts (see 3–13) and *income receipts on assets* (5–4), which is the sum of interest (see 3–20), dividends (see 2–22), and reinvested earnings on U.S. direct investment abroad (see 2–23).

Account 6. Domestic Capital Account

This account presents gross saving and the statistical discrepancy on the right side and "gross domestic investment, capital transfers, and net lending" on the left.

Gross saving (6–18) is net saving plus the consumption of fixed capital (see 1–11). *Net saving* (6–8) is calculated as the sum of personal saving (see 3–8), undistributed corporate profits with inventory valuation and capital consumption adjustments (see 2–17), private wage accruals less disbursements (see 1–4), and net government saving (see 4–10). It supplements the NIPA gross saving measure and provides a useful measure of the saving that is available for adding to the Nation's net stock of fixed assets.

Statistical discrepancy (see 1–13).

Gross domestic investment (6–1) measures the total investment in the United States in fixed assets (that is, the structures, equipment, and software that are used in production) and in inventories (change in private inventories). It is the sum of private fixed investment (see 1–20), government fixed investment (see 1–29), and change in private inventories (1–25).

Capital accounts transactions (net) (6–5) consist of capital transfers (mainly debt forgiveness and migrants' transfers) and the transfers of nonproduced nonfinancial assets to (or from) the rest of the world.

Net lending or net borrowing (–), national income and product accounts (6–6) is equal to the balance on current account less capital accounts transactions (net). It may be viewed as an indirect measure of the net acquisition of foreign assets by U.S. residents less the net acquisition of U.S. assets by foreign residents.

Account 7. Foreign Transactions Capital Account

The right side of this account shows capital accounts transactions (net) (see 6–5) and net lending or net borrowing (–), national income and product accounts (see 6–6). The left side shows the balance on current account, national income and product accounts (see 5–20).

Other Definitions

Final sales of domestic product is GDP less change in private inventories; equivalently, it is the sum of PCE, private fixed investment, government consumption expenditures and gross investment, and net exports of goods and services.

Gross domestic purchases is the market value of goods and services purchased by U.S. residents, regardless of where those goods and services were produced. It is GDP less net exports of goods and services; equivalently, it is the sum of PCE, gross private domestic investment, and government consumption expenditures and gross investment.

Final sales to domestic purchasers is gross domestic purchases less change in private inventories.

Net interest is the interest paid by private enterprises less the interest received by private enterprises, plus the interest paid by the rest of the world less the interest received by the rest of the world. Interest payments on mortgage and home improvement loans and on home equity loans are included in interest paid by private enterprises because home ownership is treated as a private enterprise. Interest received by private noninsured pension plans is recorded as being directly received by persons in personal income. Interest paid by nonprofits serving households is included in interest paid by private enterprises, while interest received by nonprofits serving households is included in the interest received by persons. In addition to monetary interest, net interest includes imputed interest. Imputed interest is made up of 1) imputed income paid to policy holders by property and casualty insurance companies and life insurance companies, measured as the investment income earned on policyholders' reserves; 2) implicit services provided by financial intermediaries other than commercial banks, measured as the property income received by them less the interest paid by them to business, households and institutions, governments, and the rest of the world; and 3) implicit services provided by commercial banks in the form of both depositor and borrower services.[33]

Fixed assets are produced assets that are themselves used repeatedly, or continuously, in processes of production for more than 1 year. Fixed assets consist of equipment, software, and structures (including, by convention, owner-occupied housing); consumer durable goods are not included. *Fixed investment* is the net acquisition of fixed assets.

Produced assets are nonfinancial assets that have come into existence as outputs from a production process; they include fixed assets and private inventories.

Nonproduced assets are nonfinancial assets that are used for production but have not themselves been produced; they include naturally occurring assets, such as land and mineral deposits.

Population is the total population of the United States, including the Armed Forces overseas and the institutionalized population. The monthly estimate is the average of Census Bureau survey estimates for the first of the month and the first of the following month; the quarterly and annual estimates are the averages of the relevant monthly estimates.

Personal saving as a percentage of disposable personal income (DPI), frequently referred to as "the personal saving rate," is calculated on a monthly, quarterly, and annual basis as the ratio of personal saving to DPI.

Gross saving as a percentage of gross national income (GNI), sometimes referred to as "the national saving rate," is calculated on a quarterly and annual basis as the ratio of gross saving—the sum of net saving and consumption of fixed capital—to GNI.

U.S. residents are individuals, governments, business enterprises, trusts, associations, nonprofit organizations, and similar institutions that have the center of their economic interest in the United States and that reside or expect to reside in the United States for 1 year or more. (For example, business enterprises residing in the United States include U.S. affiliates of foreign companies.) In addition, U.S. residents include all U.S. citizens who reside outside the United States for less than 1 year and U.S. citizens residing abroad for 1 year or more who meet one of the following criteria: Owners or employees of U.S. business enterprises who reside abroad to further the enterprises' business and who intend to return within a reasonable period; U.S. Government civilian and military employees and members of their immediate families; and students who attend foreign educational institutions.

Foreign residents are those residing and pursuing economic interests outside the United States. They also include international institutions located in the United States, foreign nationals employed by their home governments in the United States, and foreign affiliates of U.S. companies.

The rest of the world consists of foreign residents who are transactors with U.S. residents.

REAL OUTPUT AND RELATED MEASURES

In addition to estimating the current-dollar market value of GDP, BEA estimates "real," or inflation-adjusted, GDP and its components.

Quantity and Price Indexes

BEA's chain-type quantity and price indexes, in combination with the current-dollar estimates, provide users with the basic data series from which all other analytical tables and presentations of the NIPAs are derived.

Changes in current-dollar GDP measure the changes in the market value of the goods, services, and structures produced in the economy in a particular period. These changes can be decomposed into quantity and price components that, in turn, can be expressed as index numbers with the reference year—at present, the year 2000—equal to 100. These are referred to as "chain-type" indexes. Percent changes in real GDP and its components are equal to the percent changes of the quantity indexes; percent changes in prices are equal to the percent changes of the price indexes.[34]

The annual changes in quantities and prices in the NIPAs are calculated using a Fisher formula that incorporates weights from 2 adjacent years. For example, the 2003–04 change in real GDP uses prices for 2003 and 2004 as weights, and the 2003–04 change in prices uses quantities for 2003 and 2004 as weights.[35] These annual changes are "chained" (multiplied) together to form time series of quantity and price indexes. Quarterly changes in quantities and prices are calculated using a Fisher formula that incorporates weights from two adjacent quarters; quarterly indexes are adjusted for consistency to the annual indexes before percent changes are calculated. (For more details, see appendix 1, "Formulas for Calculating Chain-Type Quantity and Price Indexes.")

The Fisher formula produces percent changes in quantities and prices that are not affected by the choice of reference year. In addition, the use of the Fisher formula has several other advantages over fixed-weighted measures: (1) It eliminates substitution bias in real GDP growth that tends to cause an understatement of growth for periods before the reference year and an overstatement of growth for periods after the reference year; (2) it eliminates the distortion of growth in components and in industries that result from the fixed- weighted indexes; and (3) it eliminates the anomalies that arise from using recent-period price weights to measure periods in the past when a far different set of prices prevailed.[36]

Chained-Dollar Measures

BEA also prepares measures of real GDP and its components in a dollar-denominated form, designated "chained (2000) dollar estimates." For GDP and most other series, these estimates are computed by multiplying the current-dollar value in 2000 by a corresponding quantity index number and then dividing by 100. For example, if a current-dollar GDP component equaled $100 in 2000 and if real output for this component increased 15 percent by 2004, then the chained (2000) dollar value of this component in 2004 would be $115 (= $100 x 115/100). (For a list of the chained- dollar series that are not calculated in this way, see appendix 2, "Chained Measures in the NIPAs Not Calculated as Fisher Indexes.")

The chained (2000) dollar, or "real," estimates provide measures to calculate the percent changes for GDP and its components that are consistent with those calculated from the chain-type quantity indexes; any differences will be small and due to rounding. For most components of GDP, the chained-dollar estimates also provide rough approximations of their relative importance and of their contributions to real GDP growth for years close to 2000.[37] However, for some components—such as computers and other high-tech equipment with rapid growth in real sales and falling prices—chained-dollar levels (as distinct from chain- weighted indexes and percent changes) overstate the relative importance of such components to GDP growth.[38]

In addition, chained-dollar values for the detailed GDP components will not necessarily sum to the chained-dollar estimate of GDP (or any intermediate aggregate) because the relative prices used as weights for any period other than the reference year differ from those used for the reference year. BEA provides a measure of the extent of such differences by showing a “residual” line on chained-dollar tables that indicates the difference between GDP (or other major aggregate) and the sum of the most detailed components in the table.

For periods close to the reference year, when there usually has not been much change in the relative prices that are used as the weights for calculating the chain-type index, the residuals tend to be small, and the chained (2000) dollar estimates can be used to approximate the contributions to growth and to aggregate the detailed estimates.

Contributions

For periods further from the reference year, the residual tends to become larger, and the chained-dollar estimates are less useful for analyses of contributions to growth.[39] For this reason, BEA also shows contributions of major components to the percent change in real GDP (and to the percent change in other major aggregates) that use exact formulas for attributing growth. (For details, see appendix 3, “Calculation of Component Contributions to the Change in GDP and Other Major Aggregates.”)

The contributions tables have table numbers with the format #.#.2, and the presentation is limited to the contributions to the percent change in GDP (or in another major aggregate) from the preceding year or quarter. For some analytical purposes, it may be desirable to calculate contributions to growth for more than a single quarter or year or to calculate contributions to growth for aggregates not shown in these tables. An article in the SURVEY provides information on how to prepare chained-dollar series with different reference years that permit the calculation of close approximations of contributions to real growth for any period.[40] The article shows how to calculate a chained-dollar series for any period by using the percent changes in the chain-type indexes to compute chained-dollar series indexed to the current dollars of whatever reference year is appropriate for the analysis. In the article, different reference years are used depending upon the time period analyzed; for example, for decades and business cycles, the midpoints of the periods are used.[41]

Current-Dollar Shares

Two tables show the percentage shares of GDP and GDI that are accounted for by major components. These shares, which are calculated on a current-dollar basis, provide data users with an accurate measure of the size and importance of the components of GDP and GDI. Table 1.1.10, which shows the shares of GDP, is published annually and quarterly, and table 1.11, which shows the shares of GDI, is published annually.

Price Indexes

BEA's featured aggregate price measure is the price index for gross domestic purchases, which measures the prices paid for goods and services *purchased* by U.S. residents. This index is derived from the prices of PCE, gross private domestic investment, and government consumption expenditures and gross investment. In contrast, the GDP price index measures the prices paid for goods and services *produced* by the U.S. economy and is derived from the prices of PCE, gross private domestic investment, net exports, and government consumption expenditures and gross investment. Thus, the two indexes differ with respect to coverage of the prices of exported and imported goods and services. Price changes in goods and services produced abroad and sold in the United States are reflected in the gross domestic purchases measure but not in the GDP measure; price changes in goods and services produced by the U.S. economy and sold abroad are reflected in the GDP price measure but not in the gross domestic purchases price measure. For example, a change in the price of imported petroleum that is fully passed on to U.S. consumers would be fully reflected in the price index for gross domestic purchases but not in the GDP price index, because imports are subtracted in deriving GDP.

Implicit Price Deflators

BEA also prepares another price index, the implicit price deflator (IPD), which is calculated as the ratio of the current-dollar value to the corresponding chained- dollar value, multiplied by 100 (see appendix 1, "Formulas for Calculating Chain-Type Quantity and Price Indexes"). The values of the IPD are very close to the values of the corresponding chain-type price index for all periods. IPDs for GDP and its major components are presented as index numbers in NIPA table 1.1.9.

Command-Basis GNP and Terms of Trade

BEA also prepares another measure of "real" output—*command-basis GNP* (tables 1.8.3 and 1.8.6). Command-basis GNP is a measure of the goods and services produced by the U.S. economy in terms of their purchasing power. GNP and command-basis GNP differ in how their real values are prepared: In estimating real GNP, the current-dollar values of the detailed components of exports of goods and services are deflated by export prices, the current-dollar values of the detailed components of imports of goods and services are deflated by import prices, and the current- dollar value of most factor income is deflated by the IPD for final sales to domestic purchasers. In estimating command-basis GNP, the current-dollar value of the sum of exports of goods and services and of income receipts is deflated by the IPD for the sum of imports of goods and services and of income payments.

The *terms of trade* is a measure of the relationship between the prices that are received by U.S. producers for exports of goods and services and the prices that are paid by U.S. purchasers for imports of goods and services. When the terms of trade improve (that is, when export prices rise relative to import prices), the purchasing power, or command value of U.S. GNP in international markets, increases by more than the production of goods and services valued in U.S. prices. Conversely, when the terms of trade deteriorate (that is, when export prices fall relative to import prices), the purchasing power, or command value of U.S. GNP in international markets, increases by less than the production of goods and services valued in U.S. prices.

The terms of trade is measured by the following ratio, with the decimal point shifted two places to the right: In the numerator, the IPD for the sum of exports of goods and services and of income receipts; in the denominator, the IPD for the sum of imports of goods and services and of income payments. Changes in the terms of trade reflect the interaction of several factors, including movements in exchange rates, changes in the composition of traded goods and services, and changes in producers' profit margins. For example, if the U.S. dollar depreciates against a foreign currency, a foreign manufacturer may choose to absorb this cost by reducing the profit margin on the product it sells to the United States, or it may choose to raise the price of the product and risk a loss in market share.

Classifications of Production

In the NIPAs, production is classified by type of product, by sector, by legal form of organization, and by industry.

Type of Product

Type of product classifications—goods (durable and nondurable), services, and structures—are presented for GDP and the components of final sales of domestic product.

Goods are tangible products that can be stored or inventoried, services are products that cannot be stored and are consumed at the place and time of their purchase, and structures are products that are usually constructed at the location where they will be used and that typically have long economic lives. In cases in which a product has characteristics of more than one of these classifications (for example, restaurant meals), or in which source data do not provide detail on type of product (for example, foreign travel), the product is classified on the basis of the dominant characteristic.

Accordingly, the following products are included in goods: Restaurant meals; expenditures abroad by U.S. residents except for travel (for example, expenditures of U.S. military and embassy personnel abroad); replacement parts whose installation cost is minimal; dealers' margins on used equipment; and movable household appliances, such as refrigerators, even when they are included in the purchase price of a new home.

The following products are included in services: Food that is included in airline transportation and hospital charges; natural gas and electricity (except in exports and imports); goods and services that are included in current operating expense of nonprofit institutions (for example, office supplies); foreign travel by U.S. residents; expenditures in the United States by foreigners; repair services, which include the cost of parts (except replacement parts whose installation cost is minimal); defense research and development; and exports and imports of certain goods, primarily military equipment purchased and sold by the Federal Government.

Government consumption expenditures for the Federal Government and state and local governments are recognized as services produced by general government. The value of these services, most of which are not sold in the market, are measured by the cost of inputs: Compensation, consumption of fixed capital (CFC), and intermediate goods and services purchased less own-account investment and sales to other sectors. (Purchases by general government of goods and services are classified as intermediate purchases.)

The following products are included in structures: Manufactured homes; certain types of installed equipment, such as elevators, heating, and air conditioning systems; brokers' commissions on sale of structures; architectural and engineering fees included in the value of structures; land development costs; and mining exploration, shafts, and wells.

In PCE, in exports, in imports, and in government intermediate goods and services purchased, durable goods have an average life of at least 3 years. In fixed investment, equipment and software consists of goods that have an average life of at least 1 year. In change in private inventories, goods held by manufacturing and trade establishments are classified as durable goods or nondurable goods in accordance with the classification of the industry of the establishment holding the inven tories. Inventories held by construction establishments are classified as durable goods. Inventories held by establishments other than those in manufacturing, trade, and construction are classified as nondurable goods.

Sector

In the NIPAs, a breakdown of GDP is also shown in terms of the three sectors of the economy—business, households and institutions, and general government; the term "value added" refers to the product of sectors.

Business: Production by all entities that produce goods and services for sale at a price intended at least to approximate the costs of production, corporate and noncorporate private entities organized for profit, and certain other entities that are treated as business in the NIPAs. These entities include mutual financial institutions, private noninsured pension funds, cooperatives, nonprofit organizations (that is, entities classified as nonprofit by the Internal Revenue Service (IRS) in determining income tax liability) that primarily serve business, Federal Reserve banks, federally sponsored credit agencies, and government enterprises.[42] Gross value added of the business sector is measured as GDP less the gross value added of households and institutions and of general government.[43]

Households and institutions: The households and institutions sector comprises households and nonprofit institutions serving households (NPISHs). The gross value added of households is measured by the services of owner-occupied housing and the compensation paid to domestic workers. The gross value added of NPISHs is measured by the compensation paid to the employees of these institutions, the rental value of fixed assets owned and used by these institutions, and the rental income of persons for tenant-occupied housing owned by these institutions.

General government: The government sector comprises all Federal Government and state and local government agencies except government enterprises. The gross value added of general government is measured as the sum of the compensation of the employees of these agencies and of their CFC.

Legal Form of Organization

For the domestic business sector, income and its components are shown for corporate business and noncorporate business. Noncorporate business, in turn, comprises sole proprietorships and partnerships, other private business, and government enterprises (employee compensation and current surplus of enterprises).

Corporate business: This legal form comprises all entities required to file Federal corporate tax returns (IRS Form 1120 series). These entities include mutual financial institutions and cooperatives subject to Federal income tax, nonprofit institutions that primarily serve business, Federal Reserve banks, and federally sponsored credit agencies.

Sole proprietorships: This legal form comprises all entities that would be required to file IRS Schedule C (Profits or Loss from Business) or Schedule F (Farm Income and Expenses) if the proprietor met the filing requirements.

Partnerships: This legal form comprises all entities required to file Federal partnership income tax returns, IRS Form 1065 (U.S. Partnership Return of Income).

Other private business: This legal form comprises all entities that would be required to report rental and royalty income on the individual income tax return in IRS Schedule E (Supplemental Income and Loss) if the individual met the filing requirements, tax-exempt cooperatives, and buildings and equipment and software owned and used by NPISHs.

Government enterprises: This legal form consists of government agencies that cover a substantial proportion of their operating costs by selling goods and services to the public and that maintain their own separate accounts. A "mixed" treatment of government enterprises is used in the NIPAs: Some types of transactions are recorded as if they were part of the business sector, and others are recorded as if they were part of the general government sector. The following transactions of government enterprises are treated like those of businesses and included in the NIPA business sector: (1) Their sales to final users are recorded as sales by businesses, (2) their purchases of materials and business services are considered intermediate, and (3) their compensation payments and CFC are deducted in calculating their income. Within the business sector, government enterprises are classified as noncorporate businesses.

Other transactions of government enterprises are treated like those of other government agencies: (1) Their interest payments are combined with those of general government rather than those of business, (2) their investment in equipment and software and in structures is combined with general government investment rather than with business investment in gross private domestic investment, and (3) their profit-like income, the current surplus of government enterprises (see definition on page 9), accrues to general government.

Industry

Industrial distributions are presented for national income and its components, capital consumption allowances, employment and hours, and the change in private inventories and the stock of private inventories.[44] For the estimates of income and employment by industry beginning with 1998, the classification underlying the distributions of private activities is based on the North American Industrial Classification System (NAICS).[45] For the estimates of inventories beginning with the first quarter of 1997, the estimates are also based on NAICS. For estimates before these dates, the industry classifications are based on the Standard Industrial Classification (SIC).[46]

The industry distributions in most of the tables in "Income and Employment" (table section 6; see Presentation of the NIPAs below) are shown as follows: Estimates for 1929–48 based on the 1942 SIC are shown in tables designated as part A; estimates for 1948–87 based on the 1972 SIC are shown as part B; estimates for 1987–2000 based on the 1987 SIC are shown as part C; and estimates for 1998 forward are based on the 1997 NAICS are shown as part D. The industry distributions based on the 1997 NAICS reflect the corresponding shift of most of the NIPA source data to a NAICS basis. The estimates for earlier years have not been adjusted to the 1997 NAICS basis because of a lack of adequate source data. Instead, the estimates for 1948 are shown on the basis of both the 1942 and 1972 SIC, the estimates for 1987 are shown on the basis of both the 1972 and the 1987 SIC, and the estimates for 1998–2000 are shown on the basis of both the 1987 SIC and the 1997 NAICS.

Industrial distributions of government activities are not provided; instead, they are combined into a single category. For most series, separate estimates are shown for the activities of the Federal Government, of state and local governments, and of government enterprises. Expenditures by the Federal Government and by state and local governments are also shown by type and by function.

The industrial distributions for private activities are based on data collected from "establishments" or from "companies" (also called enterprises, or firms). Establishments are economic units, generally at a single physical location, where business is conducted or where services or industrial operations are performed (for example a factory, mill, store, hotel, movie theater, mine, farm, airline terminal, sales office, warehouse, or central administrative office). Companies consist of one or more establishments owned by the same legal entity or group of affiliated entities. Establishments are classified into an industry on the basis of their principal product or service, and companies are classified into an industry on the basis of the principal industry of all their establishments. Because large multiestablishment companies typically own establishments that are classified in different industries, the industrial distribution of the same economic activity on an establishment basis can differ significantly from that on a company basis. For example, employment of steel-manufacturing companies differs from employment of steel-manufacturing establishments because the employment of these companies includes the employment of establishments that are not classified in steel manufacturing and because it excludes the employment of establishments that manufacture steel but are not owned by steel-manufacturing companies.

Industrial distributions on a consistent establishment or company basis are not available for all NIPA components. As a result, the industrial distribution of national income reflects a mix of establishment and company data. For the following series, the industrial distributions are based on establishment data: Compensation of employees, employment, hours, inventories, rental income of persons, farm proprietors' income, farm net interest, and farm noncorporate capital consumption allowances. For nonfarm proprietors, industrial distributions of proprietors' income, net interest, and capital consumption allowances are based on company data; these data are regarded as being substantially the same as if they were based on establishment data because nearly all unincorporated companies own only one establishment (and the few multiestablishment companies usually own establishments in the same industry). For corporations, industrial distributions of profits, nonfarm net interest, and capital consumption allowances are based on company data.

In addition, individual industry series are not fully comparable over time. Historical comparability is affected primarily by two factors. First, the composition of industries may change because of changes in the NAICS or SIC basis that is used for the estimates. This factor affects estimates based on establishment data and on company data.

Second, historical comparability is affected because the industrial classification of the same establishment or company may change over time. This factor affects company-based estimates much more than establishment-based estimates. The classification of a company may change as a result of the following: Shifts in the level of consolidation of entities for which company reports are filed; mergers and acquisitions; and other shifts in principal activities, especially for large, diversified firms.

In addition to the industrial distributions of private activities, some NIPA tables show the following special industry groupings:

Financial industries consists of the following NAICS industries: Finance and insurance, and management of companies and enterprises. Finance and insurance consists of Federal Reserve banks; credit intermediation and related activities; securities, commodity contracts, and investments; insurance carriers and related activities; and funds trusts, and other financial vehicles. Management of companies and enterprises consists of bank and other holding companies.

Nonfinancial industries consists of all other private industries.

Goods-producing industries consists of the following NAICS divisions: Natural resources (agriculture, forestry, fishing, and hunting) and mining; construction; and manufacturing.

Services-producing industries consists of the following NAICS divisions: Wholesale trade, retail trade, transportation and warehousing, and utilities; and other services-producing industries (information; finance and insurance; real estate and rental and leasing; professional, scientific, and technical services; management of companies and enterprises; administrative and waste management services; educational services; health care and social assistance; arts, entertainment, and recreation; accommodation and food services; and other services, except government).

PRESENTATION OF THE NIPAS

This section describes the release schedule for the NIPA estimates, the publication of the NIPA tables, and additional presentations of NIPA and NIPA related estimates.[47]

Release Schedule

For GDP and most other NIPA series, quarterly estimates are released on the following schedule: "Advance" estimates are released near the end of the first month after the end of the quarter; as more detailed and more comprehensive data become available, "preliminary" and "final" estimates are released near the end of the second and third months, respectively.

For gross national product, gross domestic income, national income, corporate profits, and net interest, "advance" estimates are not prepared, because of a lag in the availability of source data. Except for the fourth quarter estimates, the initial estimates for these series are released with the preliminary GDP estimates, and the revised estimates are released with the final GDP estimates. For the fourth quarter, these estimates are released only with the final GDP estimates.

In addition, when the preliminary estimates of GDP for the current quarter are released, BEA releases revised estimates of private wages and salaries and affected income-side aggregates for the previous quarter.[48] This permits the incorporation of the most recently available wage and salary data from the quarterly census of employment and wages.

Monthly estimates of personal income and outlays are released near the end of the month following the reference month; estimates for the preceding 2 to 4 months are subject to revision at that time.

Annual revisions of the NIPAs are usually carried out each summer and cover the months and quarters of the most recent calendar year and of the 2 preceding years. These revisions are timed to incorporate newly available major annual source data.[49]

Comprehensive revisions are carried out at about 5- year intervals. They incorporate definitional, statistical, and presentational improvements.

Publication of the NIPA Tables

Tables that present the NIPA estimates appear each month under "National Data" in the section "BEA Current and Historical Data" in the SURVEY OF CURRENT BUSINESS and on BEA's Web site.[50] The full set of NIPA tables consists of 299 tables that present annual, quarterly, and monthly estimates.

With the release of the 12th comprehensive revision of the NIPAs, the presentation of the NIPA tables was organized to group tables with similar formats in one section of the NIPA tables. To assist users in identifying the type of estimate in a table, a numbering system for NIPA tables was developed for groups of tables that display different types of estimates using similar formats. The table-numbering system highlights the type of estimate (such as current dollars, quantity indexes, and percent changes) in the table. The new system is outlined below.

Table numbers are in the format "X.Y.Z." where "X" indicates the NIPA table section, "Y" indicates the table number in the section, and "Z" indicates the type of estimate presented.

The table sections are numbered as follows:

1 Domestic Product and Income
2 Personal Income and Outlays
3 Government Current Receipts and Expenditures
4 Foreign Transactions
5 Saving and Investment
6 Income and Employment by Industry
7 Supplemental Tables
8 Seasonally Unadjusted Estimates

The table numbers within each section are numbered sequentially. The types of estimates are numbered as follows:

1 Percent change from preceding period in real estimates (most at annual rates)
2 Contributions to percent change in real estimates
3 Real estimates, quantity indexes
4 Price indexes
5 Current dollars
6 Real estimates, chained dollars
7 Percent change from preceding period in prices
8 Contributions to percent change in prices
9 Implicit price deflators
10 Percentage shares of GDP

For example, GDP is presented in table group 1.1; the current-dollar estimates are presented in table 1.1.5, and the chained-dollar estimates are presented in table 1.1.6.

The tables that present current-dollar estimates, but not other types of estimates, use only the first two terms of the numbering system. For example, table 3.1, "Government Current Receipts and Expenditures," that presents only current-dollar estimates is not numbered 3.1.5.

For some tables, a letter suffix following the table number indicates that there are different versions of the table for different time periods; for example, table 4.3A shows the relation of foreign transactions in the NIPAs to the corresponding items in the international transactions accounts for the period 1946–85, and table 4.3B shows the same relation (with additional detail) beginning with 1986.

Most of the full set of NIPA tables are published in the issues of the SURVEY that describe the annual and comprehensive revisions (for example, see the August 2006 SURVEY); the remaining tables are published in subsequent months. In addition, a set of "Selected NIPA Tables" is published monthly in the SURVEY; this set presents the estimates for the most recent 5 quarters and the most recent 2 years. The selected set comprises 100 tables from the first seven NIPA table sections (seasonally unadjusted estimates in the last section are compiled only once a year and thus are not included in the selected set of tables). Because the numbering system used for the full set of tables is retained in the selected set, gaps occur in the numbering of the selected tables.

A note preceding the NIPA tables indicates information on the vintage of the estimates. In general, the NIPA tables in the SURVEY present estimates for the most recent 2–4 years. Historical annual and quarterly estimates for summary NIPA series are presented annually in the SURVEY and cover the following: Current- and chained-dollar GDP for most of the components in NIPA tables 1.1.5 and 1.1.6 and for final sales of domestic product and gross national product; NIPA chained-type quantity indexes in NIPA table 1.1.3 and chain-type price indexes and implicit price deflators in NIPA tables 1.1.4 and 1.1.9; and most of the major components of national income and personal income in NIPA tables 1.12 and 2.1. For example, these estimates were published as "GDP and Other Major NIPA Series, 1929–2006:II" in the August 2006 SURVEY. In addition, historical annual and quarterly estimates for the major NIPA aggregates are published monthly in table C.1 in the "BEA Current and Historical Data" section of the SURVEY.

An "Index to the NIPA Tables," which identifies the NIPA table (or tables) for each NIPA series and each topic covered by the NIPAs and which includes cross references for commonly used business and economic terms to the appropriate NIPA item was published in the May 2005 SURVEY, beginning on page 48. The index is also available on BEA's Web site in the Interactive NIPA table section.

Additional Presentations of NIPA and NIPA-Related Estimates

The SURVEY also presents the following NIPA and NIPA related estimates that do not fit neatly into the system or publication schedule for the standard NIPA presentation.

"Current-Dollar and Real Value Added by Industry" presents current- and chained-dollar estimates of value added by industry, which is the contribution of each industry including government to GDP. Estimates for value added by industry for 2002–2004 were published in the December 2005 SURVEY; advance estimates for 2005 were published in the May 2006 SURVEY. (Estimates for earlier years are available on BEA's Web site.)

"Reconciliation Table" in appendix A of the "BEA Current and Historical Data" section presents a table that reconciles NIPA estimates with related series and that provides analytically useful extensions of the NIPA estimates. This table shows the reconciliation of relevant NIPA series with related series in the international transactions accounts.

"Real Inventories, Sales, and Inventory Sales Ratios for Manufacturing and Trade," usually published in the January, April, July, and October issues of the SURVEY, shows quarterly and monthly estimates for these series. Also shown are quarterly and monthly inventories for manufacturing by stage of fabrication. Historical estimates for these series, quarterly for 1997:I–2003:IV, were published in the April 2004 SURVEY, and revised and new estimates for 2001 :IV–2005:II were published in the October 2005 SURVEY. Estimates for 1959 forward are available electronically on BEA's Web site.

"Fixed Assets and Consumer Durable Goods," usually published in the September issue of the SURVEY, shows annual estimates of net stocks for private fixed assets, government owned fixed assets, and durable goods owned by consumers. Revised and new estimates for 2003–2005 were published in the September 2006 SURVEY. Estimates for net stocks and depreciation for 1925 forward and for fixed investment for 1901 forward are available electronically on BEA's Web site. For information on how these estimates are prepared, see *Fixed Assets and Consumer Durable Goods in the United States*, 1925–97, September 2003, at <www.bea.gov/ bea/dn/Fixed_Assets_ 1925_97.pdf>.

"Selected Monthly Estimates" for personal income by type of income and for the disposition of personal income, including PCE, are published in table B.1 in the "BEA Current and Historical Data" section of the SURVEY. These estimates are also published annually in NIPA tables 2.6–2.8.6, and the estimates for the most recent months appear in the personal income and outlays news release.

"Source Data and Assumptions" shows the source data and the BEA assumptions for missing key source data that are used to prepare the advance estimates of GDP. This information is available at the time of the news release and is included in the "GDP and the Economy" articles in the SURVEY that present the advance estimates.[51]

"Reliability of the GDP Estimates" covers several articles that assess the reliability of the current quarterly estimates, which consist of the advance, preliminary, and final estimates, by comparing them with the "latest" estimates, which reflect the results of both annual and comprehensive revisions. The most recent study, which was conducted in 2005 for the period 1983–2002, found that the current quarterly estimates correctly indicated the direction of change 98 percent of the time, correctly indicated the acceleration or deceleration of aggregate economic activity about three- fourths of the time, and successfully identified whether GDP growth was high relative to trend about two- thirds of the time and whether it was low relative to trend about three-fifths of the time. For business cycles occurring during the period 1969–2002, the quarterly estimates of real GDP indicated the cyclical peaks in all five of the recessions and indicated the cyclical troughs in three of the five recessions; the two missed troughs were within one quarter of the latest estimates of the troughs.[52]

"Underlying Detail Tables" includes 62 tables that show additional information or detail underlying the NIPA estimates. These tables provide more detailed or higher frequency estimates of NIPA series that appear in the NIPA tables published elsewhere on BEA's Web site and in the SURVEY. BEA does not include these detailed estimates in the published tables because their quality is significantly less than that of the higher level aggregates in which they are included. Compared to these aggregates, the more detailed estimates are more likely to be either based on judgmental trends, on trends in the higher level aggregate, or on less reliable source data. Most of the underlying tables are updated one working day after the monthly GDP releases.

Statistical Conventions Used for NIPA Estimates

Most of the NIPA estimates are presented in current dollars. Changes in current-dollar estimates measure the changes in the market values of goods or services that are produced or sold in the economy. For many purposes, it is necessary to decompose these changes into price and quantity components. Prices are expressed as index numbers with the reference year at present, the year 2000 equal to 100. Quantities, or "real" measures, are expressed as index numbers with the reference year (2000) equal to 100; for selected series, they are also expressed in chained (2000) dollars. (For further details, see the section "Real Output and Related Measures.")

Seasonal Adjustment

Quarterly and monthly NIPA estimates are seasonally adjusted at the detailed series level when the series demonstrate statistically significant seasonal patterns. For most of the series that are seasonally adjusted by the source agency, BEA adopts the corresponding seasonal adjustment factors. Seasonal adjustment removes from the time series the average effect of variations that normally occur at about the same time and in about the same magnitude each year—for example, weather and holidays. After seasonal adjustment, cyclical and other short term changes in the economy stand out more clearly.

Annual Rates

Quarterly and monthly NIPA estimates in current and chained dollars are presented at annual rates, which show the value that would be registered if the rate of activity measured for a quarter or a month were maintained for a full year. Annual rates are used so that periods of different lengths—for example, quarters and years—may be easily compared. These annual rates are determined simply by multiplying the estimated rate of activity by 4 (for quarterly data) or by 12 (for monthly data).

Percent changes in the estimates are also expressed at annual rates. Calculating these changes requires a variant of the compound interest formula,

$$r = \left[\left(\frac{GDP_t}{GDP_0} \right)^{m/n} - 1 \right] \times 100$$

where

r	is the percent change at an annual rate;
GDP_t	is the level of activity in the later period;
GDP_0	is the level of activity in the earlier period;

m is the periodicity of the data (for example, 1 for annual data, 4 for quarterly, or 12 for monthly); and

n is the number of periods between the earlier and later periods (that is, *t–0*).

Appendix 1. Formulas for Calculating Chain-Type Quantity and Price Indexes

This appendix shows the basic calculations used to prepare annual and quarterly chain-type quantity and price indexes.

Annual Indexes

The formula used to calculate the annual change in real GDP and other components of output and expenditures is a Fisher index (*Qt F*) that uses weights for 2 adjacent years (years *t–1* and *t*). The formula for real GDP in year t relative to its value in year *t–1* is

$$Q_t^F = \sqrt{\frac{\Sigma p_{t-1} q_t}{\Sigma p_{t-1} q_{t-1}} \times \frac{\Sigma p_t q_t}{\Sigma p_t q_{t-1}}}$$

where the *p*'s and *q*'s represent prices and quantities of detailed components in the 2 years.

Because the first term in the Fisher formula is a Laspeyres quantity index (Q_t^L),

or

$$Q_t^L = \frac{\Sigma p_{t-1} q_t}{\Sigma p_{t-1} q_{t-1}}$$

and the second term is a Paasche quantity index

(Q_t^P),

or

$$Q_t^P = \frac{\Sigma p_t q_t}{\Sigma p_t q_{t-1}}$$

the Fisher formula can also be expressed for year *t* as the geometric mean of these indexes as follows:

$$Q_t^F = \sqrt{Q_t^L \times Q_t^P}.$$

The percent change in real GDP (or in a GDP component) from year *t–1* to year *t* is calculated as

$$100\,(Q_t^F - 1.0).$$

which is the geometric mean of a Laspeyres price index (P_t^L) and a Paasche price index (P_t^P), or

$$P_t^F = \sqrt{P_t^L \times P_t^P}.$$

The chain-type quantity index value for period *t* is $I_t^F = I_{t-1}^F \times Q_t^F$, and the chain-type price index is calculated calculated analogously. Chain-type real output and price indexes are presented with the reference year (b) equal to 100; that is, $I_b = 100$.

The current-dollar change from year *t–1* to year *t* expressed as a ratio is equal to the product of the Fisher price and quantity indexes:

$$\frac{\Sigma p_t q_t}{\Sigma p_{t-1} q_{t-1}} = \sqrt{\frac{\Sigma p_t q_{t-1}}{\Sigma p_{t-1} q_{t-1}} \times \frac{\Sigma p_t q_t}{\Sigma p_{t-1} q_t}} \times \sqrt{\frac{\Sigma p_{t-1} q_t}{\Sigma p_{t-1} q_{t-1}} \times \frac{\Sigma p_t q_t}{\Sigma p_t q_{t-1}}} = P_t^F \times Q_t^F .$$

Quarterly Indexes

The same formulas are used to calculate the quarterly indexes except that quarterly data are substituted for annual data.

All quarterly chain-type indexes for completed years that have been included in an annual or comprehensive revision are adjusted so that the quarterly indexes average to the corresponding annual index. When an additional year is completed between annual revisions, the annual index is computed as the average of the quarterly indexes, so no adjustment is required to make the quarterly and annual indexes consistent. For example, until the 2006 annual revision was released, the chain-type indexes for the year 2005 were computed as the average of the four quarterly indexes for 2005.

Chained-Dollar Estimates

The chained-dollar value CD_t^F is calculated by multiplying the index value by the reference year currentdollar value $(\Sigma p_b q_b)$ and dividing by 100.[53] For period *t*,

$$CD_t^F = \Sigma p_b q_b \times I_t^F / 100.$$

Implicit Price Deflators

The implicit price deflator IPD_t^F for period t is calculated as the ratio of the current-dollar value to the corresponding chained-dollar value, multiplied by 100, as follows:

$$IPD_t^F = \frac{\Sigma p_t q_t}{CD_t^F} \times 100$$

APPENDIX 2. CHAINED MEASURES IN THE NIPAS NOT CALCULATED AS FISHER INDEXES

The Fisher formula described in Appendix 1, "Formulas for Calculating Chain-Type Quantity and Price Indexes," is generally preferred for calculating the chain-type quantity and price indexes presented in the NIPAs. In the preferred method, chained dollars are obtained by multiplying the Fisher quantity index by the reference-year current-dollar value and dividing by 100. However, when the components of an aggregate include large negative values, the Fisher formula may require taking the square root of a negative number.

For these aggregates, another method for calculating chained dollars must be used. The inability to calculate a particular Fisher quantity index (for example, change in private inventories) because of negative values usually does not extend to the calculation of higher level aggregates (for example, quantity indexes for gross private domestic investment and for GDP can be computed). The calculation of contributions to percent change is not affected by negative values, so they can be calculated for all components.

The following paragraphs describe the cases for which the Fisher formula cannot be used.

For change in private inventories (in tables 1.1.6, 1.2.6, 1.4.6, 1.5.6, 5.2.6, 5.6.6A, 5.6.6B, 7.2.6B, and 7.3.6), chained-dollar series are calculated as the difference between end of period and beginning of period chain-weighted stocks of inventories. The following chained-dollar series are calculated as the current-dollar value of the series divided by an appropriate implicit price deflator: Gross national income and gross domestic income (in table 1.7.6); command-basis exports of goods and services and income receipts from the rest of the world (in table 1.8.6); and disposable personal income (in tables 2.1 and 2.6).

For the following series, real values are calculated as the sum of, or the difference between, chained-dollar series measuring flows: Net exports of goods and services (in tables 1.1.6, 1.5.6, and 4.2.6); command-basis gross national product (in table 1.8.6); net value added of nonfinancial corporate business (in table 1.14); foreign travel and other, net (in table 2.5.6); net foreign travel and net foreign remittances (in table 2.4.6); Federal nondefense intermediate purchases of durable goods, of nondurable goods, and of Commodity Credit Corporation inventory change (in table 3.10.6); Federal defense intermediate purchases of other durable goods (in table 3.11.6); net investment by major type (in table 5.2.6); residential and nonresidential private net purchases of used structures (in table 5.4.6A and 5.4.6B); Federal defense and nondefense net purchases of used structures (in table 5.8.6A and 5.8.6B); and net exports of motor vehicles (in table 7.2.6B).

For the following series, quantity indexes are calculated by dividing the chained-dollar series by its reference year (that is, 2000) value and multiplying by 100: Command-basis GNP and command-basis exports of goods and services and receipts from the rest of the world (in table 1.8.3); and income receipts from the rest of the world (in table 4.2.3).

APPENDIX 3. CALCULATION OF COMPONENT CONTRIBUTIONS TO THE CHANGE IN GDP AND OTHER MAJOR AGGREGATES

The contributions to percent change in a real aggregate, such as real GDP, provide a measure of the composition of growth in the aggregate that is not affected by the nonadditivity of its components This property makes contributions to percent change a valuable tool for economic analysis. The contribution to percent change $(C\%\Delta_{i,t})$ in an aggregate in period t that is attributable to the quantity change in component i is defined by the formula

$$C\%\Delta_{i,t} = 100 \times \frac{\left(\left(p_{i,t}/P_t^F\right) + p_{i,t-1}\right) \times (q_{i,t} - q_{i,t-1})}{\Sigma_j\left(\left(p_{j,t}/P_t^F\right) + p_{j,t-1}\right) \times q_{j,t-1}},$$

where

P_t^F is the Fisher price index for the aggregate in period *t* relative to period *t–1*;

p i,t is the price of the component *i* in period *t;* and

q i,t is the quantity of the component *i* in period *t*.

The summation with subscript *j* in the denominator includes all the deflation level components of the aggregate.

Contributions of subaggregates (such as PCE goods) to the percent change of the aggregate (say, PCE or GDP) are calculated by summing the contributions of all the deflation level components contained in the subaggregate. For annual estimates, no adjustments are required for contributions to sum exactly to the percent change in the aggregate. For quarterly estimates, adjustments are required to offset the effects of adjustments made to published aggregates and their quarterly percent change: namely, conforming quarterly estimates to average to the corresponding annual estimates, and expressing percent change at annual rate. The same formula is used for both annual and quarterly estimates of contributions to percent change in all periods. The only variation in the method of calculation is that when the annual contributions for the most recent year are first calculated, they are based on a weighted average of the quarterly contributions until the next annual revision.

REFERENCES

[1] Commission of the European Communities, International Monetary Fund, Organisation for Economic Co-operation and Development, United Nations, and the World Bank, *System of National Accounts 1993 (SNA 1993)* Brussels/Luxembourg, New York, Paris, and Washington, DC, 1993.

[2] See Charles Ian Mead, Karin E. Moses, and Brent R. Moulton, "The NIPAs and the System of National Accounts," SURVEY OF CURRENT BUSINESS 84 (December 2004): 17–32.

[3] The chain-type measures of real output and prices eliminate the over-statement of real GDP growth for periods after the reference year and the understatement of real GDP growth for periods before the reference year.

[4] U.S. Congress, Joint Economic Committee, Subcommittee on Economic Statistics, "The National Economic Accounts of the United States: Review,

Appraisal, and Recommendations," in *The National Economic Accounts of the United States*, report by the National Accounts Review Committee, National Bureau of Economic Research, 85th Congress, October 1957.

[5] "A Critique of the United States Income and Product Accounts." *Studies in Income and Wealth*, vol. 22. Princeton, NJ: Princeton University Press, for the National Bureau of Economic Research, 1958.

[6] "The Economic Accounts of the United States: Retrospect and Prospect," SURVEY 51 (July 1971), Part II, 50th anniversary issue.

[7] Office of Federal Statistical Policy and Standards, *Gross National Product Data Improvement Project Report*, report of the Advisory Committee on Gross National Product Data Improvement, Washington, DC: U.S. Department of Commerce, 1977.

[8] Murray F. Foss, ed., "The U.S. National Income and Product Accounts: Selected Topics," *Studies in Income and Wealth*, vol. 47, Chicago: University of Chicago Press, for the National Bureau of Economic Research, 1983.

[9] Comptroller General, *The Bureau of Economic Analysis Should Lead Efforts to Improve GNP Estimates* (Washington, DC: General Accounting Office, 1982).

[10] "Mid-Decade Strategic Review of BEA's Economic Accounts: Maintaining and Improving Their Performance," SURVEY 75 (February 1995): 36–66, and "Mid-Decade Strategic Review of BEA's Economic Accounts: An Update," SURVEY 75 (April 1995): 48–56.

[11] Dale W. Jorgenson, J. Steven Landefeld, and William D. Nordhaus, eds., "A New Architecture for the U.S. National Accounts," *Studies in Income and Wealth*, vol. 66, Chicago: University of Chicago Press, for the National Bureau of Economic Research, 2006.

[12] Prior to the 2003 comprehensive revision, the NIPAs were summarized in five accounts, which are shown in table A of the August 2002 SURVEY on pages 38–39. For a discussion of the differences between the old and new summary accounts, see Nichole Mayerhauser, Shelly Smith, and David F. Sullivan, "Preview of the 2003 Comprehensive Revision of the National Income and Product Accounts: New and Redesigned Tables," SURVEY 83 (August 2003): 8–15.

[13] For more information on the concepts underlying the accounts, see U.S. Bureau of Economic Analysis (BEA), "An Introduction to National Economic Accounting," methodology paper, forthcoming, and *SNA 1993*.

[14] The estimate of GDP avoids double counting (of, for example, the semiconductors that go into computers or the flour that goes into bread)

because the purchase by one business of materials and services on current account (intermediate purchases) from another business is canceled by the corresponding sale by another business in the consolidation.

[15] In the NIPAs, the United States consists of the 50 states (before 1960, Alaska and Hawaii were not included), the District of Columbia, and U.S. military installations, embassies, and consulates abroad.

[16] Capital gains and losses are not included in NIPA measures, because they result from the revaluation and sale of existing assets rather than from current production.

[17] Prior to the 2003 comprehensive revision, national income consisted only of "factor incomes."

[18] Inventory valuation adjustment (IVA) is the difference between the cost of inventory withdrawals valued at acquisition cost and the cost of inventory withdrawals valued at replacement cost. The IVA is needed because inventories as reported by business are often charged to cost of sales (that is, withdrawn) at their acquisition (historical) cost rather than at their replacement cost (the concept underlying the NIPAs). As prices change, businesses that value inventory withdrawals at acquisition cost may realize profits or losses. Inventory profits, a capital-gains-like element in business income (corporate profits and nonfarm proprietors' income), result from an increase in inventory prices, and inventory losses, a capitalloss-like element, result from a decrease in inventory prices. In the NIPAs, inventory profits or losses are shown as adjustments to business income; that is, they are shown as the IVA with the sign reversed. No adjustment is needed to farm proprietors' income because farm inventories are measured on a current-market cost basis. The private capital consumption adjustment (CCAdj) converts depreciation that is on a historical-cost (book value) basis—the capital consumption allowance (CCA)—to depreciation that is on a current-cost basis— consumption of fixed capital (CFC)—and is derived as the difference between private CCA and private CFC.

[19] Own-account production refers to an asset produced by a business or government for its own use.

[20] Intermediate goods also include net purchases of used goods and changes in inventories. Change in inventories is not included in government investment because source data to prepare estimates for most inventory categories are not available. At present, the estimates for a few inventory categories for which data are available, such as inventories held by the Commodity Credit Corporation and the Strategic Petroleum Reserve, are included in government consumption expenditures.

[21] Miscellaneous compensation of employees includes judicial fees paid to jurors and to witnesses, compensation of prison inmates, and marriage fees paid to justices of the peace.

[22] For years prior to 1959, subsidies is presented net of the current surplus of government enterprises (1–10), because detailed data to separate the series for this period are not available.

[23] Several asset types use depreciation patterns that are not geometric. For example, computers and peripheral equipment and private autos use actual empirical depreciation profiles, and missiles and nuclear fuel rods use a straight-line pattern. For more information on depreciation patterns, see U.S. Department of Commerce, Bureau of Economic Analysis, Fixed Assets and Consumer Durable Goods in the United States, 1925–97, (Washington, DC: U.S. Government Printing Office, September 2003) and <www.bea.gov/bea/dn/Fixed_assets_1925_97.pdf>.

[24] For additional details on the statistical discrepancy, see Robert P. Parker and Eugene P. Seskin, "Annual Revision of the National Income and Product Accounts," SURVEY 77 (August 1997): 19.

[25] Government enterprises are not included in account 2, because complete estimates on sources and uses of government enterprise income, notably the income payments and income receipts on assets, are not currently available. The sources and uses of government enterprise income are included, but not separately identified, in the government receipts and expenditures account.

[26] Summary account 2 presents the components of private enterprise income on a national basis, that is, for labor and property supplied by U.S. residents. Consequently, for the net operating surplus to be shown in account 2 on a domestic basis consistent with summary account 1, several income flows to and from the rest of the world must also be shown in account 2.

[27] *Net interest and miscellaneous payments*, a component of national income, consists of interest and miscellaneous payments (2–2) less interest receipts (2–21). For a definition of net interest, see the section "other definitions" (page 14).

[28] Interest payments on mortgage and home improvement loans and on home equity loans are included in interest paid by private enterprises because home ownership is treated as a business in the NIPAs.

[29] This treatment is consistent with the guidelines of *SNA 1993*, paragraph 7.121.

[30] The corporate profits that are associated with private noninsured pension plans are recorded as zero, and the property income is recorded as being

received directly by persons in the corresponding components of personal income.

[31] Publicly administered government employee retirement plans are classified as employee pension and insurance funds, not as government social insurance programs.

[32] Taxes from the rest of world also includes some taxes on production and some current transfers, but the source data do not permit the reliable separation of the taxes on income.

[33] Commercial banks provide implicit services to both depositors and borrowers. Depositor services are measured as the difference between the interest received by depositors and the interest they would have received had they been paid a risk-free rate of interest (reference rate). Depositors receive a lower interest rate for their deposits in exchange for the unpriced services provided by banks. Borrower services are measured as the difference between the interest paid by borrowers and the interest they would have paid had they borrowed at the reference rate. Borrowers pay a higher interest rate for loans in exchange for the unpriced services provided to them by banks. The unpriced depositor services are recorded as imputed interest paid by financial intermediaries and received by depositors. The unpriced borrower services are recorded as negative imputed interest received by the financial intermediaries and negative interest paid by borrowers. Thus, imputed interest paid by private enterprises includes the interest paid by financial intermediaries for depositor services and the negative interest paid by businesses and owner-occupied housing in their role as borrowers.

[34] Indexes are not presented for change in private inventories, for net exports, and for most of the "net" series in tables 2.4.3, 2.4.4, 2.5.3, 2.5.4, 3.9.3, 3.9.4, 5.2.3, 5.4.3, 5.4.4, 5.8.3, and 5.8.4 because indexes for these series are not meaningful.

[35] Because the source data available for most components of GDP are measured in dollars rather than in units, the quantities of most of the detailed components used to calculate percent changes are obtained by deflation. For deflation, quantities are approximated by real values (expressed, at present, with 2000 as the reference year) that are calculated by dividing the current-dollar value of the component by its price index, where the price index uses 2000 as the reference year. Two other methods, quantity extrapolation and direct valuation, are also used to calculate real values for a number of the most detailed GDP components. For quantity extrapolation, the real values are obtained by extrapolating the current-dol-

lar estimates for the reference year in both directions by quantity indicators; for example, the real values for "mining exploration, shafts, and wells structures" are extrapolated using oilwell footage drilled. For direct valuation, the real values are obtained by multiplying reference-year prices by quantity data for each period; for example, the real values of "natural gas inventories" are calculated using quantities and prices of natural gas stocks. For more information, see "Updated Summary Methodologies," in the November 2005 SURVEY.

[36] For further discussion, see J. Steven Landefeld, Brent. R Moulton, and Cindy M. Vojtech, "Chained-Dollar Indexes: Issues, Tips on Their Use, and Upcoming Changes," SURVEY 83 (November 2003): 6–16; J. Steven Landefeld and Robert P. Parker, "BEA's Chain Indexes, Time Series, and Measures of Long Term Economic Growth," SURVEY 77 (May 1997): 58–68; and Jack E. Triplett, "Economic Theory and BEA's Alternative Quantity and Price Indexes," SURVEY 72 (April 1992): 49–52.

[37] The availability of chained-dollar estimates before 1990 has been limited to key aggregates. However, detailed quantity indexes, which are accurate for all periods, are presented in tables with table numbers having format #.#.3, most of which begin with 1929. These quantity indexes can be used in place of chained-dollar estimates in analyses that require data on real GDP or its components over time, as well as to calculate percent changes. For GDP and its major components, annual growth rates beginning with 1930 and quarterly growth rates beginning with the second quarter of 1947 are presented in table 1.1.1.

[38] The problems associated with chained-dollar levels for components with rapidly changing prices is the result of using a fixed reference year in conjunction with a chain index whose weights change every period to reflect changes in relative prices. It is mathematically impossible to "force" chained-dollar levels to reflect both the current-period weights and periodto-period percent changes that are consistent with a chain index.

[39] This is why most of the chained-dollar series for detailed components are shown beginning with 1990, although chained (2000) dollar estimates for selected series for earlier periods are shown in tables 1.1.6, 1.2.6, 1.3.6, 1.4.6, 1.7.6, and 1.8.6.

[40] See Landefeld and Parker, "BEA's Chain Indexes," 63–66.

[41] NIPA tables 1.1.6A, 1.1.6B, 1.1.6C, and 1.1.6D present annual estimates of real GDP and its major components in chained (1937) dollars, chained (1952) dollars, chained (1972) dollars, and chained (1982) dollars, respectively. However, users should be aware that contributions calculated

from these tables are approximations and may produce misleading results for periods far from those reference years or when relative prices are changing rapidly, such as during the energy crisis of 1973–75.

[42] For more detail on government enterprises, see the section "Legal form of organization."

[43] Gross value added of financial and of nonfinancial corporations are also shown in the NIPA tables. They are calculated based on the costs incurred and the incomes earned from production.

[44] An industrial distribution of fixed investment based on data collected from establishments is prepared as part of the procedure used to estimate fixed assets. For further information, see *Fixed Assets and Consumer Durable Goods in the United States, 1925–97* (Washington, DC: U.S. Government Printing Office, September 2003). Industrial distributions of gross output, intermediate inputs, and gross product are also prepared; for further information, see Brian C. Moyer, Mark A. Planting, Paul V. Kern, and Abigail M. Kish, "Improved Annual Industry Accounts for 1998–2003: Integrated Annual Input-Output Accounts and Gross-Domestic-Product-by-Industry Accounts," SURVEY 84 (June 2004): 21–57; Robert E. Yuskavage and Yvon H. Pho, "Gross Domestic Product by Industry for 1987–2000: New Estimates on the North American Industry Classification System," SURVEY 84 (November 2004): 33–53; and George M. Smith, Matthew J. Gruenberg, Tameka R.L. Harris, and Erich H. Strassner, "Annual Industry Accounts: Revised Estimates for 2001–2003," SURVEY 85 (January 2005): 9–43.

[45] See Executive Office of the President, Office of Management and Budget, *North American Industry Classification System, United States, 1997* (Washington, DC: Bernan Press, 1998).

[46] See Office of Management and Budget, Statistical Policy Division, *Standard Industrial Classification Manual, 1987* (Washington, DC: U.S. Government Printing Office (GPO), 1988); Office of Management and Budget, Statistical Policy Division, *Standard Industrial Classification Manual, 1972* (Washington, DC: GPO, 1972); and Bureau of the Budget, *Standard Industrial Classification Manual, 1942* (Washington, DC: GPO, 1942).

[47] For additional details on the availability of BEA's products and services, see BEA's Web site at <www.bea.gov>.

[48] Affected aggregates include gross domestic income, the statistical discrepancy, gross national income, national income, personal income, disposable personal income, personal saving, gross (national) saving,

compensation, and gross product of corporate business. Other components that are closely linked to wages and salaries, such as personal current taxes and employer contributions for government social insurance are also revised. However, GDP and its components are not affected.

[49] For a discussion of the most recent annual revision of the NIPAs, see Eugene P. Seskin and Shelly Smith, "Annual Revision of the National Income and Product Accounts," SURVEY 86 (August 2006): 7–31.

[50] The NIPA estimates appear first in news releases, which are available to the general public in a variety of forms.

[51] Additional information about source data and assumptions is also available on BEA's and STAT-USA's Web sites.

[52] See Dennis J. Fixler and Bruce T. Grimm, "Reliability of the NIPA Estimates of U.S. Economic Activity," SURVEY 85 (February 2005): 8–19 and Bruce T. Grimm and Teresa L. Weadock, "Gross Domestic Product: Revisions and Source Data," SURVEY 86 (FEBRUARY 2006): 11–15.

[53] For exceptions to this procedure, see appendix 2.

In: Measuring the Economy: GDP and NIPAs
Editor: Kemal Sahin
ISBN: 978-1-60741-199-4
© 2009 Nova Science Publishers, Inc.

Chapter 4

THE TREATMENT OF FEDERAL RECEIPTS AND EXPENDITURES IN THE NATIONAL INCOME AND PRODUCT ACCOUNTS*

Congressional Budget Office

PREFACE

This article describes how the treatment of federal receipts and expenditures in the national income and product accounts differs from the recording of federal revenues and outlays in the federal budget, as prepared by the Office of Management and Budget. It is one of a series of reports that the Congressional Budget Office (CBO) issues each year to fulfill section 202(e) of the Congressional Budget Act of 1974, which requires CBO to submit to the Committees on the Budget periodic reports about fiscal policy and to provide baseline projections of the federal budget. Most recently, in response to that requirement, CBO issued *The Budget and Economic Outlook: An Update* (August 2008).

Frank Russek of CBO's Macroeconomic Analysis Division and Barry Blom of CBO's Budget Analysis Division wrote the article under the supervision of Robert Dennis and Peter Fontaine. Loretta Lettner edited the article, and Maureen Costantino prepared it for publication. Lenny Skutnik printed copies of the article,

* This is an edited, excerpted and augmented edition of a Congressional Budget Office publication.

Linda Schimmel handled the print distribution, and Simone Thomas prepared the electronic version for CBO's Web site (www.cbo.gov).

Peter R. Orszag
Director

September 2008

The fiscal transactions of the federal government are recorded in two major sets of accounts that conceptually are quite different. The framework generally used by executive branch agencies and the Congress, and typically discussed in the press, is the one presented in the *Budget of the United States Government,* which is prepared by the Office of Management and Budget. The budget focuses on cash flows—revenues (funds generated by collecting taxes and imposing certain fees) and outlays (cash disbursed for the various federal functions). The objectives of the budget are to provide information that can assist lawmakers in their policy deliberations, facilitate the management and control of federal activities, and help the Treasury manage its cash balances and determine its borrowing needs.

The national income and product accounts (NIPAs) also record the federal government's fiscal transactions, but as an accounting device, they have different objectives. Produced by the Bureau of Economic Analysis (BEA), an agency within the Department of Commerce, the NIPAs are intended to provide a comprehensive measure of activity in the U.S. economy—specifically, current production (the process by which goods and services are provided for consumption) and the income generated by that production.[1] A well-known measure of production in the NIPAs is gross domestic product (GDP). The accounts, which are used extensively in macroeconomic analysis, divide the economy into four major sectors— business, government, household, and the "rest of the world" (the foreign sector)—each with its own set of accounts.[2] The federal sector, which is the focus of this article, is one component of the government sector (the state and local sector is the other component).[3] Because the aims of the NIPAs differ from those of the federal budget, the two accounting systems treat some government transactions very differently.

CONCEPTUAL DIFFERENCES BETWEEN THE FEDERAL BUDGET AND THE FEDERAL SECTOR IN THE NIPAS

The budget of the federal government is best understood as an information and management tool. It focuses primarily on cash flows, recording the inflow of revenues and the outflow of spending over a given period. The period of foremost interest in the budget is the federal fiscal year, which runs from October 1 through September 30. A few exceptions to the general rule of recording transactions on a cash basis exist, but they are designed to improve the usefulness of the budget as a decisionmaking tool. For example, when the federal government makes direct loans or provides loan guarantees (as with student loans), tracking cash flows gives a misleading view of current costs; therefore, under what is termed credit reform, the budget records the estimated subsidy costs at the time the loans are made.

The federal sector of the NIPAs reflects none of the planning and management goals that underlie the budget. Instead, it illustrates how the federal government fits into a general economic framework, detailing current production and income over specific periods, the major sources of that production, and recipients of income resulting from output. The time increments considered in the NIPAs are primarily calendar years and calendar quarters, although approximate totals for fiscal years can be derived from the quarterly estimates. (The tables in this Web document show fiscal year numbers.)

From the perspective of the NIPAs, the federal government is both a producer and a consumer. Its workforce uses purchased goods and services and government- owned capital (buildings, equipment, and software) to produce services for the public at large; because those services are consumed by the public, that consumption, by convention, is regarded as a federal expenditure in the NIPAs. In addition, through its taxes and transfers, the federal government affects the resources available to the private sector. The purpose of the NIPAs is to record all of those activities consistently.

The federal sector of the NIPAs tracks how much the government spends on the consumption of goods and services, and it records the transfer of resources that occurs through taxation, payments to the beneficiaries of federal programs, and federal interest payments. The federal sector's contribution to GDP is presented elsewhere in the NIPAs (Table 1.1.5 in the accounts).

DIFFERENCES IN RECORDING MAJOR TRANSACTIONS

The conceptual differences that distinguish the NIPAs from the federal budget lead to accounting differences as well. In attempting to properly incorporate federal transactions into the framework used to determine GDP, the NIPAs reflect judgments about how to best treat transactions such as government investment, the sale and purchase of existing assets, federal credit, and federal activities that resemble those of businesses, as well as transactions involving U.S. territories. In some cases, the appropriate treatment may be to move a transaction from the federal sector to another section of the NIPAs or to exclude the transaction from the NIPAs entirely. In other cases, the appropriate treatment may involve recording as a receipt in the NIPAs an item that the federal budget reports as an offsetting (negative) budget outlay or adjusting the timing of a federal transaction to better match the timing of related production or income flow.[4]

The Measurement of National Saving

Several conventions used in the NIPAs are intended to show the federal government's contribution to national saving—specifically, net federal government saving (current receipts minus current expenditures). Two major departures from the federal budget are the treatment of spending for federal investment (for things such as ships, computers, and office buildings) and the treatment of spending for federal employees' retirement programs. As a result, the concept of net federal saving in the NIPAs is akin to, but not the same as, the federal budget surplus.

Federal Investment

In the federal budget, outlays for investment are treated like other cash outlays; thus, to determine the size of the federal deficit or surplus, they are subtracted from budget revenues. By contrast, in the NIPAs, federal investment is not counted as a current expenditure (and therefore does not affect net federal government saving) because new purchases of federal capital (investments) do not measure the current capital inputs used to produce government services.[5] To approximate the cost of those capital inputs, the NIPAs include in current federal expenditures an estimate of the depreciation (consumption of fixed capital) of the stock of federal capital. The treatment is conceptually similar to that applied to the corporate business sector, which uses depreciation rather than investment purchases to compute net corporate saving (retained earnings). In the federal budget, depreciation is not tracked. Table 1, which provides a crosswalk between CBO's most recent baseline budget projections and the NIPAs, shows that difference in coverage in the row labeled "Treatment of Investment and Depreciation."[6]

Federal Retirement

Transactions involving federal employees' retirement programs are also handled differently in the budget and in the NIPAs. In the budget, federal employees' contributions to their retirement accounts are recorded as revenues; agencies' contributions on behalf of their employees (as well as interest payments from the Treasury to trust funds) have no overall budgetary effect because they simply represent transfers of funds between two government accounts.[7] Benefit payments to federal retirees are recorded as outlays in the budget. By contrast, in the NIPAs, the aim is to make the measurement of saving by the federal government consistent with that of the private sector. Therefore, the NIPAs treat some of the transactions related to federal retirement plans as part of the household sector.[8] The receipts from federal employers' retirement contributions (and the interest earned by retirement accounts) are considered part of workers' personal income and thus are not recorded as federal transactions (receipts or negative expenditures). Employees' contributions are not recorded as income in either the federal or the household sector but are considered transfers within the household sector.

On the outlay side, pension benefit payments to retirees are not recorded as federal expenditures in the NIPAs because they are treated as transfers from pension funds within the household sector. Some transactions, however, are treated as part of federal expenditures even though the corresponding receipts are recorded in the household sector. The government's contributions to its workers' retirement accounts are counted as federal expenditures (as part of employees' compensation), as is the interest paid to federal retirement accounts.[9] The different treatment of retirement contributions by federal employees is shown in the top section of Table 1 under the column heading "Receipts"; the different treatment of federal employers' contributions, interest earnings, and benefit payments is shown below that, under "Expenditures."

Table 1. Differences Between the Federal Budget and the National Income and Product Accounts as Reflected in CBO's Baseline Projections (Billions of dollars, by fiscal year)

	Actual											
	2007	2008	2009	2010	2011	2012	2013	2014	2015	2016	2017	2018
						Receipts						
Revenues (Budget)[a]	2,568	2,548	2,720	2,881	3,178	3,451	3,619	3,770	3,958	4,145	4,341	4,546
Differences												
Coverage												
Contributions for government												
employees' retirement	-4	-4	-4	-4	-4	-4	-3	-3	-3	-3	-3	-3
Estate and gift taxes	-26	-29	-27	-21	-20	-54	-62	-69	-75	-81	-87	-94
Geographic adjustments	-5	-5	-5	-5	-6	-6	-6	-6	-7	-7	-7	-7
Universal Service Fund receipts	-8		-8	-9	-9	-9	-9	-10	-10	-10	-10	-10
Subtotal, coverage	-43	-46	-45	-40	-39	-73	-81	-88	-94	-101	-108	-115
Netting												
Medicare premiums	50	54	60	60	62	65	70	75	80	85	91	98
Deposit insurance premiums	*	1	4	4	5	5	3	*	*	*	*	*
Government contributions for												
OASDI and HI for employees	16	17	18	19	20	21	22	23	24	26	27	28
Income receipts on assets	21	23	27	29	30	30	33	33	33	33	32	34

	Actual											
	2007	2008	2009	2010	2011	2012	2013	2014	2015	2016	2017	2018
Surpluses of government enterprises	-3	-2	-8	-7	-6	-2	-6	-6	-7	-7	-8	-9
Other	31	33	35	36	36	37	38	38	39	40	41	37
Subtotal, netting	116	126	136	141	146	156	160	162	169	176	182	188
Timing shift of corporate estimated												
tax payments	3	0	0	8	3	-17	-4	10	0	0	0	0
Other adjustments[b]	-21	-3	9	-3	-4	-1	-2	2	2	3	2	2
Total Differences	55	77	100	105	107	65	73	87	76	79	77	76
Receipts in the NIPAs	2,624	2,625	2,820	2,987	3,284	3,516	3,692	3,857	4,034	4,223	4,417	4,622
						Expenditures						
Outlays (Budget)[a]	2,729	2,955	3,158	3,312	3,502	3,577	3,766	3,939	4,120	4,352	4,514	4,680
Differences												
Coverage												
Treatment of investment and												
depreciation	-19	-22	-24	-26	-28	-29	-29	-29	-30	-30	-31	-32
Contributions for government												
employees' retirement	35	58	50	53	56	59	63	67	72	77	82	88
Capital transfers	-50	-52	-54	-57	-59	-60	-62	-63	-64	-65	-66	-66
Lending and financial												
adjustments	29	33	-11	6	11	10	9	9	10	10	11	11
Geographic adjustments	-15	-16	-17	-18	-19	-19	-21	-22	-23	-24	-25	-26
Universal Service Fund	-7	-8	-8	-9	-9	-9	-9	-9	-9	-10	-10	-10

Table 1. (Continued).

	Actual											
	2007	2008	2009	2010	2011	2012	2013	2014	2015	2016	2017	2018
Subtotal, coverage	-27	-7	-65	-50	-48	-48	-48	-46	-44	-42	-39	-36
Netting												
Medicare premiums	50	54	60	60	62	65	70	75	80	85	91	98
Deposit insurance premiums	*	1	4	4	5	5	3	*	*	*	*	*
Government contributions for												
OASDI and HI for employees	16	17	18	19	20	21	22	23	24	26	27	28
Income receipts on assets	21	23	27	29	30	30	33	33	33	33	32	34
Surpluses of government enterprises	-3	-2	-8	-7	-6	-2	-6	-6	-7	-7	-8	-9
Other	31	33	35	36	36	37	38	38	39	40	41	37
Subtotal, netting	116	126	136	141	146	156	160	162	169	176	182	188
Timing adjustments	8	-2	0	0	-31	30	1	0	0	-43	-4	47
Other Adjustments[c]	6	-28	-22	-16	-17	-15	-14	-9	-7	-5	-12	-12
Total Differences	103	89	49	74	51	123	99	108	119	87	128	187
Expenditures in the NIPAs	2,832	3,045	3,207	3,386	3,553	3,700	3,865	4,047	4,238	4,439	4,643	4,867
				Net Federal Government Saving								
Budget Deficit[a]	-161	-407	-438	-431	-325	-126	-147	-170	-162	-207	-174	-135

	Actual											
	2007	2008	2009	2010	2011	2012	2013	2014	2015	2016	2017	2018
Differences												
Coverage												
Treatment of investment and depreciation	19	22	24	26	28	29	29	29	30	30	31	32
Contributions for government employees' retirement	-39	-62	-54	-57	-60	-63	-67	-71	-75	-80	-85	-91
Estate and gift taxes	-26	-29	-27	-21	-20	-54	-62	-69	-75	-81	-87	-94
Capital transfers	50	52	54	57	59	60	62	63	64	65	66	66
Lending and financial adjustments	-29	-33	11	-6	-11	-10	-9	-9	-10	-10	-11	-11
Geographic adjustments	10	11	12	13	13	14	14	15	16	17	18	19
Universal Service Fund	*	*	*	*	*	*	*	*	*	*	*	*
Subtotal, coverage	-16	-39	20	11	9	-25	-33	-42	-50	-59	-69	-79
Timing adjustments	-6	2	0	8	34	-48	-4	10	0	43	4	-47
Other adjustments[b]	-27	25	31	13	13	14	12	11	8	8	14	15
Total Differences	-48	-12	51	31	56	-58	-26	-21	-42	-9	-52	-111
Net Federal Government Saving[d]	-208	-420	-387	-400	-269	-184	-172	-190	-204	-216	-225	-245

Source: Congressional Budget Office. For details on CBO's baseline budget projections, see *The Budget and Economic Outlook: An Update* (September 2008).

Note: * = between -$500 million and $500 million; OASDI = Old-Age, Survivors, and Disability Insurance; HI = Hospital Insurance.

[a] Includes Social Security and the Postal Service.

[b] Includes timing differences not shown elsewhere in Table 1, plus discrepencies between figures in the NIPAs and in the budget that may diminish when the Bureau of Economic Analysis makes subsequent revisions. The figure for 2007 reflects netting adjustments for hurricane relief and recovery.

[c] Includes coverage differences not shown elsewhere above.

[d] Net federal saving or dissaving is akin to the federal surplus or deficit in the budget. Negative numbers here indicate dissaving.

Capital Transfers and Exchanges of Existing Assets

Transactions that involve existing assets do not affect the way current production and income are measured in the NIPAs. Therefore, the NIPAs do not count capital transfers or asset exchanges as part of current federal receipts or expenditures, although the budget generally does include those transactions. The NIPAs define as capital transfers—and thus exclude—estate and gift taxes (which are taxes on private-capital transfers) and investment grants to state and local governments (for air transportation, highways, transit, and water treatment plants).[10] Exchanges of existing assets include federal transactions for deposit insurance and the sale and purchase of government assets (including assets that are not "produced," such as land and licenses to use the radio spectrum). Those differences between the NIPAs' federal sector and the budget accounts appear as estate and gift taxes on the revenue side of Table 1and as capital transfers and lending and financial adjustments on the outlay side.

Credit Programs

For federal credit programs (loans and loan guarantees), only the estimated credit subsidy and administrative costs are included in outlays. Cash flows from loan disbursements, repayments, and interest, by contrast, are reported in what are termed financing accounts, which have no effect on outlays.

As in the budget, the NIPAs record administrative costs and generally exclude loan disbursements and repayments and other cash flows that are considered exchanges of existing assets or financial and lending transactions that are unrelated to current production. The NIPAs do not record subsidy costs. In another departure from the budget, the NIPAs include the interest receipts from credit programs (as part of federal receipts). Those differences in the treatment of credit programs are recorded in two places in Table 1: Under the heading "Expenditures," the figures in the row labeled "Lending and Financial Adjustments" show the differences in the way loan subsidies are handled; under "Receipts," the difference in the treatment of loan interest is captured as part of "Income Receipts on Assets."

Geographic Coverage

The NIPAs exclude all government transactions with Puerto Rico and other U.S. territories, whose current production, as defined in the NIPAs, is not part of the nation's GDP. Because federal transfers dominate those transactions, their exclusion tends to increase the NIPAs' depiction of net federal government saving by comparison with the budget's measure of saving—the federal deficit or surplus. That difference in coverage is shown as geographic adjustments in Table 1.

Universal Service Fund

The business activity of the Universal Service Fund, which provides resources to promote access to telecommunications, is recorded in the budget but not in the NIPAs' federal sector. The Universal Service Fund receives federally required payments from providers of interstate and international telecommunications services and disburses those funds to local providers that serve high-cost areas, low-income households, libraries, and schools, as well as to rural health care providers. The fund is administered by the Universal Service Administrative Company, an independent nonprofit corporation regulated by the Federal Communications Commission.

Although the Universal Service Fund's revenues and outlays appear in the federal budget, they have little net effect on the deficit or surplus. In the NIPAs, the fund's receipts and payments are classified as intracorporate transfers (from one business to another within the corporate sector). The difference in treatment of the Universal Service Fund is so labeled in Table 1.

Interest Receipts

In the NIPAs, federal interest receipts are grouped with other types of federal receipts (in the category designated "Income Receipts on Assets") rather than netted against federal interest payments as they are in the federal budget.[11] BEA's treatment is consistent with international accounting practices, wherein interest receipts and payments are reported separately. The difference in the treatment of interest receipts in the NIPAs and in the federal budget raises the NIPAs' measure of government receipts relative to federal budget revenues and increases the NIPAs' measure of federal spending relative to budget outlays. However, because the difference in treatment affects receipts and expenditures in the NIPAs by exactly the same amount, it has no effect on the NIPAs' measurement of net federal government saving.

Surpluses of Government Enterprises

In the NIPAs, the surpluses (or deficits) recorded by certain government enterprises, such as the Postal Service, are shown on a separate line as current receipts of the federal government. That treatment is in keeping with international accounting standards, which generally advocate reporting spending on a gross, rather than a net, basis. By contrast, surpluses of government enterprises are treated as offsetting receipts in the federal budget.

Military Sales and Assistance in-Kind

Because the NIPAs try to identify contributions to GDP by sector, they do not classify as part of federal consumption purchases by the military of equipment and services that are intended for sale or as gifts to foreign governments. Instead, those transactions are considered net exports in the NIPAs' foreign-transactions account (Table 14.1 in the accounts). In the case of gifts, the transactions also are recorded in the federal sector of the NIPAs as a portion of transfers to the rest of the world— a classification that parallels their treatment in the federal budget, where they are categorized as outlays. By contrast, even though the cost of acquiring military equipment that is then sold to foreign governments is recorded in the federal budget as outlays, the proceeds from those sales are recorded as offsetting receipts.

Timing Differences

As much as is possible, the NIPAs attempt to measure income flows when income is earned (on an accrual basis) rather than when income is received (on a cash basis).[12] For example, BEA attributes corporate tax payments to the year in which the liabilities are incurred rather than to the time when the payments are actually made. That approach makes sense in an integrated system of accounts that tracks both production and income because on an accrual basis—measurement problems aside—the value of what is produced in a given period should match the total income generated. However, the NIPAs are not entirely consistent in that respect: Personal tax payments are counted as they are made and are not attributed retroactively to the year in which the liabilities were incurred. Because the budget is recorded mostly on a cash basis and the NIPAs' federal sector is recorded largely on an accrual basis, the timing of recorded transactions differs in several areas.

Corporate Taxes

Legislation sometimes temporarily shifts the timing of corporate tax payments (usually from the end of one fiscal year to the beginning of the next, or vice versa). The NIPAs exclude such timing shifts, which are not consistent with accrual accounting. Timing adjustments for the net effects of enacted legislation are shown in Table 1 under the heading "Receipts" in the row labeled "Timing Shift of Corporate Estimated Tax Payments."

Although corporations make estimated tax payments throughout the year, any shortfalls (or overpayments) are corrected in the form of final payments (or refunds) in subsequent years. Whereas the federal budget records those final payments on a cash basis, the NIPAs shift them back to the year in which the corporate profits that gave rise to the tax liabilities were actually generated. The results of that difference are difficult to identify for recent history and thus appear under the heading "Receipts" in Table 1 in the "Other Adjustments" category.[13]

Personal Taxes

Although personal taxes are not recorded on an accrual basis in the NIPAs, BEA nevertheless attempts to avoid large, distorting upward or downward spikes in personal disposable income that result from timing quirks. Such quirks occur each year in April, for example, when most final settlements for the previous year's personal taxes are paid. In the NIPAs, therefore, those settlements are evenly spread over the four quarters of the calendar year in which they are paid. (As with accrual accounting, that treatment avoids spikes. Unlike accrual accounting, however, it does not move payments back to the year in which the liabilities were incurred.) Such "smoothing" can alter the relationship of the NIPAs and the budget accounts for various fiscal years because it shifts some receipts into the last quarter of the calendar year and thus into the following fiscal year.[14]

Again, those adjustments are difficult to identify for recent history and thus are not shown separately in Table 1. They appear instead under "Receipts" in the row labeled "Other Adjustments."

Transfers and Military Compensation

Timing adjustments are needed on the spending side of the NIPAs to align military compensation and government transfer payments—for example, veterans' benefits, Supplemental Security Income (SSI) payments, and Medicare's payments to providers—with income that is reported on an accrual basis in the NIPAs. Misalignments can occur because of accelerations in the timing of payments that result from quirks in the calendar (holidays and weekends or leap years) or because of legislation designed to delay payments.

SSI payments and veterans' benefits are usually disbursed on the first day of each month, but if the first of the month falls on a weekend or holiday, payments are made a day or more in advance. If that occurs for the October benefits, payments are pushed into the previous fiscal year in the budget. In such cases, the NIPAs introduce a timing adjustment that effectively moves the payments back to the first day of the month. Hence, the NIPAs' adjustment always ensures that there are exactly 12 monthly SSI payments in a year, whereas in the budget, there may be 11 in some years and 13 in others.

For military compensation, which is normally paid at the beginning and middle of each month but may sometimes, like SSI, be paid early to avoid weekends, the adjustment in the NIPAs always ensures 24 payments in a year. In the budget, by contrast, there may be 23 payments in some years and 25 in others. Under the heading "Expenditures" in Table 1, the row labeled "Timing Adjustments" reflects that regularizing for transfers and for military pay.

In another contrast with the federal budget, the NIPAs record Medicare payments on an accrual basis rather than on a cash basis.[15] That treatment better illustrates the link between the underlying economic activity (the medical services provided) and the associated federal transactions (payment for those services), which can be several months apart. The timing adjustment, however, has only a small effect on the NIPA measure of net federal government saving.

Business Activities

Both the federal budget and the NIPAs treat certain revenues as offsetting receipts when they result from voluntary transactions with the public that resemble business activities, such as proceeds from the sale of government publications. However, the NIPAs generally have a stricter view of what resembles a business transaction. In particular, Medicare premiums, deposit insurance premiums, rents, royalties, and regulatory or inspection fees are deemed equivalent to business transactions in the budget but not in the NIPAs.

Consequently, those transactions (negative outlays in the budget) are treated in the NIPAs as government receipts (contributions for government social insurance and current transfers from business— such as fines and fees, and taxes on production and imports). Those differences are recorded within the category "Netting" in Table 1. Because they affect total current receipts and total current expenditures by exactly the same amounts, they have no effect on the NIPAs' measure of net federal government saving.

Presentation of the Federal Government's Receipts and Expenditures in the NIPAs

As in the budget, the federal sector of the NIPAs classifies receipts by type, but the categories differ (see Table 2). The NIPAs' classifications help determine measures such as disposable income and corporate profits after taxes. There are five major categories of current receipts. The largest category, current tax receipts, includes taxes on personal income, corporate income, and production and imports (excise taxes and customs duties), as well as taxes from the rest of the world. The next-largest category— contributions for government social insurance—consists of Social Security taxes, Medicare taxes and premiums, and unemployment insurance taxes. The remaining categories are current transfer receipts (fines and fees), income receipts on assets (interest, rents, and royalties), and current surpluses of government enterprises (such as the Postal Service).

In the NIPAs, the government's expenditures are classified according to purpose. The major groups, which are fewer than in the federal budget, are consumption expenditures, or spending on goods and services, including the costs of capital depreciation (with separate estimates for defense and nondefense spending); transfer payments (to individuals, state and local governments, and the rest of the world); interest payments; and subsidies to businesses and government enterprises.

Consumption of goods and services (for defense and nondefense purposes) consists of spending by the government for immediate use in production. (The largest portion of such consumption is the compensation of military and civilian federal employees.) Among the government's consumption expenditures, the consumption of fixed capital—depreciation—represents a partial measure of the services the government receives from its stock of fixed assets, such as buildings or equipment.

Table 2. CBO's Baseline Projections of Receipts and Expenditures as Measured in the National Income and Product Accounts' Framework

(Billions of dollars)	Actual											
	2007	2008	2009	2010	2011	2012	2013	2014	2015	2016	2017	2018
Receipts												
Current Tax Receipts												
Taxes on personal income	1,142	1,152	1,269	1,365	1,568	1,712	1,824	1,922	2,026	2,136	2,250	2,372
Taxes on corporate income	373	320	344	355	376	389	396	408	420	435	449	464
Taxes on production and imports	98	98	100	102	110	115	119	122	126	131	135	136
Taxes from the rest of the world	15	15	14	15	17	18	19	20	21	23	24	25
Subtotal	1,627	1,587	1,728	1,837	2,071	2,235	2,359	2,472	2,594	2,724	2,859	2,997
Contributions for Government												
Social Insurancea	934	968	1,015	1,067	1,127	1,186	1,239	1,291	1,344	1,399	1,457	1,518
Current Transfer Receipts	37	40	47	50	52	55	55	55	57	60	63	66
Income Receipts on Assets	29	32	38	40	41	42	45	45	46	47	46	49
Current Surpluses of Government Enterprises	-3	-2	-8	-7	-6	-2	-6	-6	-7	-7	-8	-9
Total Current Receipts	2,624	2,625	2,820	2,987	3,284	3,516	3,692	3,857	4,034	4,223	4,417	4,622
Expenditures												
Consumption Expenditures (Purchases of Goods and Services)												
Defense												
Consumption	494	537	594	633	655	673	689	706	723	742	760	780

Table 2. (Continued).

(Billions of dollars)	Actual											
	2007	2008	2009	2010	2011	2012	2013	2014	2015	2016	2017	2018
Consumption of fixed capital	75	79	81	83	85	87	90	93	95	98	100	102
Nondefenseb												
Consumption	244	260	276	288	295	302	311	322	331	341	351	360
Consumption of fixed capital	29	30	30	31	31	31	32	32	33	33	34	34
Subtotal	842	906	982	1,035	1,065	1,093	1,121	1,153	1,182	1,214	1,245	1,276
Current Transfer Payments												
Government social benefits												
To persons	1,233	1,358	1,432	1,499	1,566	1,634	1,729	1,835	1,949	2,069	2,190	2,329
To the rest of the world	4	4	4	4		5	5	5	6	6	6	7
Subtotal	1,237	1,362	1,436	1,503	1,570	1,639	1,734	1,840	1,955	2,075	2,196	2,335
Other transfer payments												
Grants-in-aid to state and local governmentsb	370	387	414	432	451	472	497	524	554	586	620	657
To the rest of the world	33	37	37	39	41	42	43	43	44	45	46	47
Subtotal	403	424	451	472	492	514	540	568	598	631	666	703
Interest Paymentsb	304	305	291	330	378	402	418	437	454	470	486	501
Subsidies	45	48	47	47	48	52	51	49	49	50	50	51
Total Current Expenditures	2,832	3,045	3,207	3,386	3,553	3,700	3,865	4,047	4,238	4,439	4,643	4,867
Net Federal Government Saving												
Net Federal Government Saving	-208	-420	-387	-400	-269	-184	-172	-190	-204	-216	-225	245

[a] Includes Social Security taxes, Medicare taxes and premiums, and unemployment insurance taxes.

[b] Includes Social Security and the Postal Service.

Source: Congressional Budget Office.

Transfer payments (cash payments made directly to individuals and the rest of the world, as well as grants to state and local governments or foreign nations) constitute another grouping. Social benefits make up most of the transfers to individuals. Grants-in-aid are payments the federal government makes to state or local governments, which generally use them for transfers (such as benefits provided by the Medicaid program) and consumption (such as the hiring of additional police officers). Current transfers to the rest of the world include federal purchases of military equipment for delivery to foreign governments.

The NIPAs' category for federal interest payments shows only payments and thus differs from the budget category labeled "Net Interest." In the NIPAs, federal interest receipts are classified with other federal receipts.

The NIPAs' category "Subsidies" primarily consists of payments by the federal government to businesses, including state and local government enterprises, such as public housing authorities. Federal housing and agricultural assistance have long dominated that category.

Net federal government saving in the NIPAs is the difference between the current receipts and the current expenditures of the federal sector.[16] It is a component of net national saving (which also includes net saving by the state and local government sector, personal saving, and corporate retained earnings) and, thus, is a partial measure of how much of the nation's income from current production is not consumed in the current period. Net federal saving (or "dissaving") is akin to the federal surplus or deficit measured in the budget. However, net federal government saving is not a good indicator of federal borrowing requirements because, unlike the budget deficit or surplus, it is not a measure of cash flows.[17]

REFERENCES

[1] The discussion of the national income and product accounts in this report generally refers to Table 3.2 in the accounts, "Federal Government Current Receipts and Expenditures," which most closely resembles the presentation in the budget. For other discussions of the NIPAs, see Department of Commerce, Bureau of Economic Analysis, "NIPA Translation of the Fiscal Year 2009 Federal Budget," *Survey of Current Business* (March 2008); and *Budget of the United States Government, Fiscal Year 2009: Analytical Perspectives.*

[2] Some accounts in the NIPAs, such as the domestic capital account (which shows saving and investment), focus on components of gross domestic

product or income rather than on a specific sector, and they bring together relevant information from all four sectors.

[3] More formally, BEA regards the federal government and state and local governments as subsectors. The treatment of state and local governments' transactions in the NIPAs closely resembles that of the federal government's transactions.

[4] The resulting differences between the numbers reported in the NIPAs and the budget are sometimes divided into three groups: coverage, timing, and netting. Although all three types of differences can affect total revenues or outlays, netting differences have no effect on the federal deficit or surplus because they affect revenues and outlays equally.

[5] Federal investment, along with private investment spending, is shown in the NIPAs in the domestic capital account, which displays saving and investment (Table 5.1 in the accounts; see also Table 3.9.5, which shows both federal investment and consumption).

[6] The estimates and the presentation of the reconciliation between the budget and the NIPAs in Table 1 are based on CBO's interpretation of the methodology used for the accounts, as detailed in Department of Commerce, Bureau of Economic Analysis, *Survey of Current Business* (June 2003), and in BEA's reconciliation of the Administration's budget for fiscal year 2009 and the accounts, as published in the *Survey of Current Business* (March 2008).

[7] In the budget, contributions by an agency to its employees' retirement accounts are considered outlays for that agency and offsetting receipts (negative outlays) elsewhere within the budget. Thus, those intragovernmental transfers result in no net outlays or receipts for the total budget. That treatment is the same as the treatment of the federal government's contributions for Social Security and Medicare for its employees.

[8] Transactions of the National Railroad Retirement Investment Trust are part of the federal sector in the NIPAs. In addition, Social Security contributions and benefit payments for private and government employees alike are recorded in the federal sector as receipts and expenditures rather than moved to the household sector.

[9] However, in the future, BEA may consider recording the annual lump-sum payments to amortize the unfunded liabilities of the military and civilian service retirement funds as a capital transfer rather than as employees' compensation. That treatment would reflect the view that such payments are

not related to current production; see “Frequently Asked Questions,” Answer ID 480, at www.bea.gov.

[10] Another type of capital transfer that BEA does not include in the NIPAs is an annual lump-sum payment from the Treasury to the Department of Defense Medicare-Eligible Retiree Health Care Fund—a trust fund that in October 2002 began to pay for benefits received by retired members of the armed forces who are eligible for Medicare and by their dependents. Those payments to the trust fund are for accrued but unfunded liabilities for benefits attributable to work performed before 2003; BEA excludes those payments from federal expenditures because they are not related to current production. Those annual payments are made by the Treasury and recorded as outlays. However, the Treasury also records offsetting receipts (negative outlays) elsewhere within the budget. Because those annual payments have no net effect on federal spending either in the NIPAs or in the budget, there is no corresponding reconciliation item in Table 1.

[11] About half of the NIPAs’ interest receipts, derived mainly from penalties on late tax payments, are recorded as revenues in the federal budget

[12] See United Nations, *System of National Accounts* (1993), paragraph 3.19, which emphasizes reporting transactions on an accrual basis. Many of the conceptual changes to the NIPAs have been based on guidelines from that U.N. document. See also Department of Commerce, Bureau of Economic Analysis, “The NIPAs and the System of National Accounts,” *Survey of Current Business* (December 2004), pp. 17–32.

[13] Other adjustments” include timing differences not shown elsewhere in Table 1, plus discrepancies between figures in the NIPAs and the budget that may diminish when BEA makes subsequent revisions.

[14] A change in the relationship between receipts in the budget and in the NIPAs is projected to occur after certain changes in tax laws, such as the changes scheduled to take effect in 2011. CBO’s baseline for revenues incorporates the assumption that those changes do, indeed, occur.

[15] Beginning with its July 2008 annual revisions, BEA has changed the way it reports Medicare prescription drug benefits. Previously, because of data limitations, BEA reported those federal expenditures on a cash basis. Now, newly available data on “incurred benefits” from the Centers for Medicare and Medicaid Services enable BEA to show federal expenditures for Medicare prescription drug benefits on an accrual basis. That treatment is now consistent with that of other Medicare benefits in the federal sector of the NIPAs.

[16] Gross federal saving—a component of gross national saving— equals net federal saving plus depreciation (consumption of fixed capital).

[17] As an addendum to the NIPAs' Table 3.2, BEA publishes a measure labeled "Net Lending or Net Borrowing," which is closer to a cash or financial measure in several ways. Like the budget, it includes investment purchases as expenditures because those purchases must be financed from current receipts or from federal borrowing. At the same time, it excludes consumption of fixed capital because those accounting charges are not a drain on current financial resources. In addition, it includes receipts from the sale of existing assets and capital transfer receipts (for example, estate and gift taxes) and capital transfer payments (for example, investment grants to state and local governments), which are not part of current receipts or expenditures in the NIPAs but do affect cash flows. Despite those adjustments, net federal lending or borrowing in the NIPAs differs from the budget deficit or surplus because of all of the other differences in timing and coverage that distinguish the NIPAs from the budget. BEA presents those differences in Table 3.18, which is similar to the presentation in Table 1.

INDEX

A

academic, 34
academics, 34
access, 60, 155
accidental, 8, 40, 104
accommodation, 124
accounting, vii, 3, 12, 27, 34, 40, 41, 42, 43, 45, 49, 51, 52, 53, 54, 57, 60, 61, 62, 65, 68, 71, 83, 84, 88, 89, 106, 146, 148, 155, 156, 157, 165
accounting standards, 156
accuracy, 24
achievement, 34
acquisitions, 75, 124
adjustment, 16, 18, 31, 58, 64, 77, 78, 94, 96, 97, 102, 104, 106, 107, 108, 130, 133, 138, 158
administrative, 20, 46, 123, 124, 154
affiliates, 17, 83, 93, 105, 113, 114
age, 40, 75, 108
agents, 54
aggregates, 3, 26, 28, 29, 88, 93, 116, 125, 127, 129, 134, 136, 141, 142
aggregation, 56, 73, 74, 75
aging, 8, 23, 104
agricultural, 162
agriculture, 124
aid, 11, 15, 45, 53, 62, 64, 69, 70, 71, 76, 95, 103, 113, 117, 161, 162
air, 102, 120, 154
Alaska, 138
alternative, 41, 42, 56
analysts, 67
annual rate, 126, 130, 136
annuals, 31
appendix, 115, 116, 117, 128, 131, 143
armed forces, 164
Armed Forces, 113
ash, 48, 147
assessment, 42
assets, 4, 8, 9, 11, 13, 16, 17, 18, 19, 20, 21, 22, 23, 35, 39, 40, 41, 42, 43, 44, 46, 47, 48, 49, 50, 52, 53, 54, 55, 56, 58, 59, 60, 63, 64, 66, 67, 68, 69, 70, 72, 73, 74, 75, 77, 78, 79, 80, 83, 84, 86, 88, 89, 93, 94, 96, 97, 98, 99, 101, 103, 104, 105, 107, 108, 109, 110, 111, 112, 113, 121, 128, 138, 139, 142, 148, 150, 152, 154, 159, 165
assumptions, 129, 143
availability, 24, 125, 141, 142

B

background information, 27
balance of payments, 35, 88, 111
balance sheet, 34, 42, 43, 56, 85
bankers, 83
banking, 90

banks, 11, 36, 37, 43, 53, 54, 84, 106, 113, 120, 121, 124, 140
base year, 88, 89
BEA, vii, 1, 2, 13, 14, 22, 24, 25, 26, 33, 34, 35, 36, 38, 69, 74, 75, 83, 85, 86, 89, 91, 104, 114, 115, 116, 117, 118, 125, 127, 128, 129, 130, 137, 156, 157, 163, 164, 165
behavior, 91
benchmark, 74
benefits, 11, 12, 18, 19, 20, 42, 43, 54, 66, 67, 69, 70, 78, 79, 97, 98, 108, 110, 158, 161, 162, 164
bias, 115
Board of Governors, 82
bonds, 4, 11, 47, 48
borrowers, 37, 90, 140
borrowing, 13, 22, 23, 24, 50, 55, 56, 59, 65, 68, 70, 76, 81, 100, 101, 112, 146, 162, 165
breakdown, 88, 120
Brussels, 82, 136
budget deficit, 162, 165
budget surplus, 20, 148
building blocks, 48
buildings, 46, 121, 147, 148, 159
Bureau of Economic Analysis, vii, viii, 1, 2, 27, 33, 34, 82, 84, 87, 137, 139, 146, 153, 162, 163, 164
Bureau of Economic Analysis (BEA), vii, 1, 2, 33, 34, 137, 146
Bureau of the Budget, 142
business cycle, 36, 116, 129
buyer, 41

C

capacity, 17, 43, 89
capital account, viii, 13, 23, 34, 48, 54, 55, 68, 72, 75, 76, 112, 162, 163
capital consumption, 16, 18, 22, 58, 59, 64, 77, 78, 81, 94, 96, 97, 100, 104, 105, 106, 107, 108, 111, 122, 123, 138
capital gains, 9, 54, 68, 90, 106, 107, 109
capital input, 148
cash flow, 34, 41, 42, 47, 48, 49, 84, 146, 147, 154, 162, 165
Cash Flow, 47, 48
cash payments, 162
category d, 155
CE, 30, 90, 99
Census, 22, 113
Census Bureau, 22, 113
charities, 5
children, 5
circular flow, 3, 4, 7, 9, 11
citizens, 83, 113
civilian, 83, 114, 159, 163
classes, 84
classification, 120, 122, 124, 156
Co, 15, 82
Columbia, 8, 39, 138
Commerce Department, 34
commercial bank, 53, 54, 84, 113
commodity, 35, 100, 124
Commodity Credit Corporation, 135, 138
community, 2, 89
compensation, 4, 5, 9, 11, 14, 17, 19, 21, 38, 51, 52, 62, 63, 65, 66, 69, 93, 94, 99, 103, 107, 108, 120, 121, 122, 139, 143, 149, 158, 159, 163
complement, 88
complexity, 90
components, 14, 18, 21, 25, 26, 35, 57, 74, 88, 89, 92, 93, 102, 104, 107, 114, 115, 116, 117, 118, 119, 121, 122, 123, 127, 129, 131, 134, 135, 136, 139, 140, 141, 143, 162
composition, viii, 2, 7, 34, 35, 87, 92, 118, 124, 135
computer software, 101
conditioning, 102, 120
Congress, 2, 136, 146
Congressional Budget Act of 1974, viii, 145
Congressional Budget Office, v, viii, 145, 153, 161
consolidation, 124, 138
construction, 73, 101, 102, 120, 124
consumer expenditure, 5
consumer price index, 90
consumers, 7, 12, 19, 117, 128
consumption, 2, 6, 8, 10, 12, 13, 14, 15, 16, 18, 19, 22, 23, 26, 30, 35, 37, 38, 39, 40,

41, 52, 58, 59, 61, 62, 64, 65, 67, 68, 69, 71, 73, 76, 77, 78, 81, 84, 86, 89, 90, 93, 94, 95, 96, 97, 98, 99, 100, 102, 104, 105, 106, 107, 108, 109, 111, 112, 113, 117, 119, 122, 123, 138, 146, 147, 148, 156, 159, 162, 163, 165
contracts, 124
control, 36, 60, 146
copyrights, 61, 106
corporate sector, 155
corporations, 11, 17, 43, 44, 48, 51, 59, 61, 75, 84, 104, 105, 106, 107, 108, 123, 142, 157
costs, 5, 7, 10, 13, 14, 17, 37, 41, 42, 43, 45, 46, 49, 51, 52, 57, 59, 62, 84, 93, 102, 103, 120, 121, 142, 147, 154, 159
costs of production, 10, 37, 45, 57, 102, 120
coverage, 20, 24, 25, 90, 117, 149, 150, 152, 153, 155, 163, 165
covering, 88
credit, 11, 41, 57, 106, 109, 120, 121, 124, 147, 148, 154
creditors, 41, 45, 48
crime, 4
currency, 43, 118
current account, 21, 22, 72, 75, 76, 80, 99, 111, 112, 138
current account balance, 75
current prices, 13
customers, 43

D

data availability, 85
debt, 17, 109, 112
debts, 44, 60, 106
deduction, 17, 21, 98, 101, 104
defense, 4, 11, 14, 15, 71, 77, 95, 102, 119, 135, 159
deficit, 20, 22, 52, 148, 153, 155, 162, 163
deficits, 72, 86, 156
definition, 36, 37, 66, 82, 90, 93, 122, 139
deflation, 91, 136, 140
delivery, 162
demand, 43, 44, 88, 102
Department of Commerce, 1, 33, 87, 137, 139, 146, 162, 163, 164
Department of Defense, 164
deposits, 4, 43, 109, 113, 140
depreciation, 8, 10, 39, 40, 42, 43, 45, 46, 48, 49, 51, 52, 54, 60, 61, 89, 104, 106, 109, 110, 128, 138, 139, 148, 151, 153, 159, 165
direct investment, 16, 21, 58, 60, 77, 80, 96, 99, 105, 111
disability, 66, 108
Disability Insurance, 153
discounts, 45, 46, 49
disposable income, 157, 159
disposition, 23, 128
dissaving, 153, 162
distribution, viii, 2, 16, 17, 60, 87, 92, 123, 142, 146
distribution of income, viii, 17, 87, 92
District of Columbia, 8, 39, 138
dividends, 11, 16, 17, 19, 21, 42, 47, 48, 52, 53, 54, 59, 61, 75, 77, 96, 105, 106, 107, 108, 109, 111
do-it-yourself, 36
domestic economy, 8, 35, 66
domestic investment, 13, 15, 22, 23, 38, 40, 73, 76, 81, 95, 98, 100, 101, 111, 112, 117, 122, 134
donations, 19, 67, 106, 109
double counting, 38, 57, 61, 65, 71, 92, 137
durable goods, 6, 39, 67, 86, 89, 113, 120, 128, 135
duties, 52, 103, 159

E

earnings, 16, 17, 21, 41, 42, 44, 45, 46, 47, 48, 49, 58, 59, 60, 66, 77, 80, 93, 96, 99, 105, 111, 149
economic activity, vii, viii, 2, 3, 5, 7, 9, 12, 17, 25, 26, 31, 34, 35, 40, 87, 89, 92, 123, 129, 158
economic growth, vii, 2
economic indicator, 89
economic institutions, 53
economic performance, 2

economics, 7
educational institutions, 83, 114
educational services, 124
electrical system, 101
electricity, 119
electromagnetic, 56
emerging issues, 90
employee compensation, 5, 17, 121
employees, 14, 15, 18, 38, 49, 50, 51, 52, 58, 63, 64, 65, 66, 69, 70, 76, 78, 83, 93, 94, 95, 97, 99, 102, 103, 107, 108, 114, 120, 121, 123, 139, 149, 150, 152, 159, 163
employers, 5, 66
employment, 2, 8, 29, 39, 74, 89, 122, 123, 125
energy, 142
enterprise, 16, 17, 48, 49, 53, 54, 57, 59, 60, 61, 63, 69, 72, 74, 92, 104, 105, 108, 112, 139
entertainment, 124
entrepreneurs, 14
entrepreneurship, 38
environment, 36
equality, 4, 23
equity, 41, 42, 43, 44, 74, 112, 139
estate tax, 68, 103
estates, 85
estimating, 5, 25, 74, 82, 89, 114, 118
exchange rate, 118
exchange rates, 118
excise tax, 52, 103, 159
exclusion, 155
Executive Office of the President, 142
exercise, 91
expenditures, viii, 7, 8, 9, 10, 11, 12, 13, 14, 15, 18, 19, 20, 26, 29, 30, 35, 37, 38, 55, 64, 65, 67, 69, 70, 71, 72, 73, 74, 76, 78, 79, 84, 88, 89, 90, 92, 95, 97, 98, 99, 101, 102, 104, 109, 110, 112, 117, 119, 131, 138, 139, 145, 148, 149, 154, 156, 159, 162, 163, 164, 165
exports, 14, 15, 21, 35, 38, 71, 73, 75, 76, 95, 98, 102, 111, 112, 117, 118, 119, 120, 135, 140, 156
extrapolation, 25, 140

F

fabrication, 128
factor incomes, 138
family, 30, 36, 66, 102
family members, 36
February, 27, 28, 85, 86, 137, 143
federal budget, viii, 145, 146, 148, 155, 156, 157, 158, 159, 164
Federal Communications Commission, 155
federal government, 146, 147, 148, 149, 155, 156, 158, 159, 162, 163
Federal Reserve, 2, 11, 35, 55, 57, 82, 84, 85, 86, 90, 92, 106, 120, 121, 124
Federal Reserve Bank, 57
Federal Reserve Board, 35, 55, 84, 85, 86, 90, 92
fees, 19, 46, 54, 59, 67, 106, 109, 120, 139, 146, 158, 159
finance, 55, 56, 68, 124
financial capital, 4, 17, 53
financial institution, 10, 57, 106, 120, 121
financial institutions, 10, 106, 120, 121
financial intermediaries, 113, 140
financial resources, 165
financing, 20, 41, 47, 71, 103, 154
fines, 19, 54, 67, 106, 109, 159
fire, 71
firms, 84, 123, 124
fiscal policy, viii, 145
fishing, 124
flexibility, 90
flow, 3, 4, 7, 9, 11, 12, 20, 21, 34, 35, 55, 84, 90, 92, 148
Flow of Funds Accounts, 82
focusing, 68
food, 66, 124
food stamp, 66
food stamps, 66
foreign direct investment, 16, 21, 58, 60, 77, 80, 96, 99, 105, 111
foreign nation, 114, 162
foreign nationals, 114
foreign travel, 119, 135
foreigners, 7, 12, 22, 35, 109, 119

forestry, 124
forgiveness, 112
fuel, 139
funding, 17
funds, 10, 11, 18, 35, 55, 57, 66, 68, 78, 84, 90, 92, 94, 97, 103, 106, 107, 108, 109, 120, 124, 140, 146, 149, 155, 163
furniture, 101

G

gambling, 37
gas, 119, 141
GDP, i, iii, v, vii, viii, 1, 2, 4, 5, 6, 7, 8, 9, 10, 12, 13, 14, 19, 21, 23, 25, 26, 28, 29, 34, 35, 37, 38, 39, 40, 48, 52, 62, 65, 67, 71, 73, 74, 82, 84, 87, 89, 93, 98, 104, 112, 114, 115, 116, 117, 119, 120, 125, 126, 127, 128, 129, 131, 132, 134, 135, 136, 137, 140, 141, 143, 146, 147, 148, 155, 156
General Accounting Office, 91, 137
generation, 41
gift, 54, 150, 153, 154, 165
gift tax, 54, 150, 153, 154, 165
gifts, 156
GNP, 9, 39, 88, 89, 91, 93, 94, 104, 118, 135, 137
goals, 147
goods and services, vii, 2, 3, 4, 5, 6, 7, 8, 10, 11, 13, 14, 15, 21, 26, 35, 36, 37, 38, 39, 41, 43, 44, 45, 46, 49, 50, 51, 52, 57, 58, 59, 61, 62, 63, 64, 65, 67, 69, 70, 71, 73, 75, 76, 80, 82, 84, 89, 90, 92, 93, 94, 95, 98, 99, 102, 110, 111, 112, 117, 118, 119, 120, 135, 146, 147, 159
government, 2, 4, 5, 7, 9, 11, 12, 13, 14, 15, 16, 17, 18, 19, 20, 21, 22, 23, 25, 29, 34, 35, 37, 38, 39, 41, 48, 52, 53, 54, 56, 57, 58, 59, 61, 63, 64, 65, 66, 67, 68, 69, 70, 71, 72, 73, 74, 75, 76, 77, 78, 79, 80, 81, 83, 88, 90, 92, 94, 95, 96, 97, 98, 99, 100, 101, 102, 103, 104, 105, 107, 108, 109, 110, 111, 112, 113, 114, 117, 119, 120, 121, 122, 123, 124, 128, 138, 139, 140, 142, 143, 146, 147, 148, 149, 150, 151, 152, 153, 154, 155, 156, 158, 159, 162, 163, 165
government budget, 72
government expenditure, 37, 90
GPO, 142
grants, 20, 55, 57, 63, 71, 103, 110, 154, 162, 165
Great Britain, 39
Great Depression, 27, 87
gross domestic product, vii, viii, 2, 34, 87, 146, 163
Gross Domestic Product, 27, 142, 143
gross investment, 14, 15, 38, 55, 56, 71, 72, 73, 76, 94, 95, 98, 101, 102, 112, 117
gross national product, 9, 39, 88, 125, 127, 135
grouping, 162
groups, 35, 126, 159, 163
growth, vii, 2, 26, 31, 36, 115, 116, 129, 135, 136, 141
growth rate, 31, 141
guidance, 1
guidelines, 36, 90, 139, 164

H

harvesting, 36
Hawaii, 138
health, 5, 17, 65, 107, 124, 155
health care, 5, 124, 155
health insurance, 65
health insurance premiums, 65
heating, 101, 102, 120
hedonic, 89
higher education, 99
high-tech, 115
highways, 110, 154
hips, 106, 121
hiring, 35, 162
home ownership, 10, 112, 139
homeowners, 11, 17, 62, 65, 104
hospital, 66, 108, 119
hotels, 101
household, 11, 16, 36, 39, 59, 61, 65, 67, 119, 146, 149, 163

household sector, 16, 149, 163
households, 5, 7, 11, 12, 13, 18, 19, 56, 61, 62, 63, 64, 65, 66, 67, 68, 69, 70, 71, 72, 73, 74, 85, 92, 94, 104, 108, 109, 112, 120, 155
housing, 5, 10, 11, 13, 17, 29, 37, 39, 62, 63, 65, 66, 68, 73, 83, 100, 102, 104, 109, 113, 120, 140, 162
human, 36
hunting, 124
hurricane, 153

I

IBM, 89
identity, 12, 43, 45, 51, 53, 54, 55
immigrants, 68
implementation, 5
import prices, 118
imports, 14, 15, 17, 20, 21, 22, 49, 50, 51, 52, 57, 58, 62, 63, 64, 65, 70, 73, 75, 76, 79, 94, 95, 98, 102, 103, 109, 111, 117, 118, 119, 120, 159, 160
imputed income, 113
inclusion, 36, 40, 69, 72
income, vii, viii, 1, 2, 3, 4, 7, 8, 9, 10, 11, 12, 13, 14, 15, 16, 17, 18, 19, 20, 21, 22, 23, 24, 27, 29, 30, 34, 35, 38, 40, 41, 42, 45, 46, 48, 49, 50, 52, 53, 54, 55, 56, 57, 58, 59, 60, 61, 62, 63, 64, 65, 66, 67, 68, 69, 70, 71, 72, 73, 74, 75, 76, 77, 78, 79, 80, 81, 84, 85, 87, 88, 90, 92, 93, 94, 95, 96, 97, 98, 99, 100, 101, 103, 104, 105, 106, 107, 108, 109, 110, 111, 112, 113, 118, 120, 121, 122, 123, 125, 127, 128, 134, 135, 138, 139, 140, 142, 145, 146, 147, 148, 149, 154, 155, 156, 157, 158, 159, 160, 162, 163
income tax, 41, 46, 48, 54, 57, 60, 61, 67, 69, 106, 107, 109, 120, 121
incomes, viii, 7, 9, 12, 13, 14, 17, 34, 85, 87, 92, 93, 106, 138, 142
index numbers, 114, 117, 129
indicators, 26, 141
indirect measure, 23, 112
industrial, 7, 123, 124, 142
industry, 7, 28, 29, 35, 39, 73, 89, 92, 119, 120, 122, 123, 124, 128
inflation, vii, 2, 3, 88, 114
infrastructure, 69
inmates, 139
inspection, 46, 106, 158
institutions, 5, 11, 12, 13, 18, 37, 56, 59, 61, 62, 63, 64, 65, 66, 68, 69, 70, 71, 72, 74, 83, 85, 92, 94, 99, 101, 104, 106, 108, 109, 113, 114, 119, 120, 121
insurance, 13, 18, 19, 20, 52, 53, 54, 62, 64, 66, 70, 78, 79, 84, 90, 94, 97, 98, 103, 105, 107, 108, 109, 113, 124, 140, 143, 150, 152, 154, 158, 159, 161
insurance companies, 53, 54, 84, 90, 113
integration, 90
interaction, 4, 118
interdependence, 4
interest rates, 37
intermediaries, 140
Internal Revenue Service, 57, 85, 120
international investment, 35
international markets, 118
International Monetary Fund, 82, 136
interpretation, 163
interstate, 155
inventories, 5, 8, 13, 15, 22, 23, 38, 40, 43, 45, 49, 50, 51, 55, 58, 72, 73, 76, 81, 84, 95, 98, 100, 101, 102, 111, 112, 113, 120, 122, 123, 128, 134, 138, 140, 141
investment, 2, 4, 5, 8, 13, 14, 15, 16, 17, 21, 22, 23, 26, 27, 29, 35, 37, 38, 39, 40, 45, 47, 50, 55, 56, 58, 59, 60, 65, 67, 68, 69, 70, 71, 72, 73, 76, 77, 80, 81, 83, 85, 88, 89, 90, 92, 94, 95, 96, 98, 99, 100, 101, 102, 105, 109, 110, 111, 112, 113, 117, 120, 122, 128, 134, 135, 138, 142, 148, 151, 153, 154, 162, 163, 165
investment spending, 163
investors, 34, 45
IRS, 120, 121

J

January, 28, 82, 128, 142
Japanese, 39
jurors, 139

L

labor, 3, 4, 6, 7, 8, 9, 13, 14, 18, 35, 36, 38, 39, 45, 46, 59, 89, 93, 94, 139
land, 43, 55, 56, 103, 113, 120, 154
law, 102, 106
law enforcement, 102
laws, 164
lead, 38, 148
legislation, 157, 158
lenders, 37
lending, 13, 22, 23, 24, 50, 55, 56, 59, 65, 70, 76, 81, 100, 101, 111, 112, 154, 165
licenses, 52, 103, 154
limitations, 61, 65, 69, 85, 164
links, 27, 56
literacy, 4
loan guarantees, 147, 154
loans, 110, 112, 139, 140, 147, 154
local government, 5, 11, 14, 19, 67, 68, 71, 74, 88, 106, 107, 108, 109, 119, 121, 123, 154, 159, 161, 162, 163, 165
location, 12, 119, 123
London, 83
long-term, 44, 45, 91
losses, 9, 19, 42, 46, 90, 105, 106, 138
low-income, 155
Luxembourg, 82, 136

M

machinery, 101
macroeconomic, 34, 146
maintenance, 10
management, 124, 146, 147
manufacturer, 118
manufacturing, 88, 120, 123, 124, 128
manufacturing companies, 123
Mariana Islands, 39, 83
market, 4, 5, 7, 10, 13, 14, 35, 37, 38, 42, 91, 93, 94, 112, 114, 118, 119, 129, 138
market prices, 5, 37, 42
market share, 118
market value, 5, 13, 35, 38, 93, 94, 112, 114, 129
markets, 62, 89, 104, 118
marriage, 139
meals, 5, 119
measurement, 5, 6, 10, 19, 149, 156
measures, vii, viii, 2, 3, 4, 5, 9, 11, 14, 17, 24, 26, 28, 29, 34, 35, 37, 38, 39, 40, 45, 47, 48, 49, 51, 52, 53, 55, 56, 57, 60, 62, 63, 65, 67, 68, 69, 71, 72, 73, 74, 75, 76, 85, 86, 87, 89, 90, 93, 99, 111, 115, 117, 129, 136, 138, 159
Medicaid, 11, 14, 19, 162, 164
medical care, 13, 65, 66, 99
medical services, 158
Medicare, 108, 150, 152, 158, 159, 161, 163, 164
mergers, 124
military, 20, 83, 108, 110, 114, 119, 138, 156, 158, 159, 162, 163
mining, 101, 120, 124, 141
misleading, 142, 147
missiles, 139
monetary policy, 2
money, 43
mortgage, 10, 62, 63, 65, 108, 109, 112, 139
motels, 101

N

national, vii, viii, 1, 2, 9, 21, 22, 23, 24, 34, 35, 36, 39, 40, 41, 42, 49, 51, 52, 53, 54, 55, 60, 61, 69, 71, 80, 81, 83, 87, 88, 89, 90, 91, 92, 93, 94, 99, 100, 101, 102, 106, 111, 112, 113, 122, 123, 125, 127, 134, 135, 138, 139, 142, 145, 146, 148, 162, 165
National Flood Insurance Program, 106
national income, vii, viii, 1, 2, 9, 21, 22, 23, 24, 34, 80, 81, 84, 87, 88, 90, 92, 93, 94,

99, 100, 101, 106, 111, 112, 113, 122, 123, 125, 127, 134, 138, 139, 142, 145, 146, 162
National Income and Product Accounts, v, 1, 27, 28, 33, 76, 82, 83, 85, 86, 95, 137, 139, 143, 145, 160
national product, 93, 94
national saving, 113, 148, 162, 165
natural, 5, 36, 53, 56, 61, 106, 119, 141
natural disasters, 5
natural gas, 119, 141
natural resources, 53, 56, 61, 106
net exports, 14, 35, 38, 73, 98, 112, 117, 135, 140, 156
net income, 45, 48, 53, 60, 90, 94
net investment, 109, 110, 135
New York, 82, 88, 136
NIPA, vii, 2, 3, 10, 12, 20, 24, 25, 27, 28, 29, 30, 31, 33, 34, 35, 39, 57, 61, 68, 72, 73, 82, 83, 85, 86, 88, 92, 111, 117, 122, 123, 124, 125, 126, 127, 128, 129, 130, 138, 141, 142, 143, 158, 162
normal, 46, 105
North America, 122, 142
nuclear, 139

O

OASDI, 150, 152, 153
obligations, 44, 45, 110
Office of Management and Budget, viii, 142, 145, 146
offshore, 56
opportunity costs, 42
organ, 49
Organisation for Economic Co-operation and Development, 27, 136
organization, 119, 142
organizations, 11, 25, 54, 57, 83, 106, 113, 120
ownership, 11, 16, 19, 36, 41, 45, 48, 83

P

paper, vii, 1, 2, 26, 27, 34, 84, 86, 137
parents, 105
Paris, 82, 136
partnership, 61, 121
partnerships, 60, 66, 106, 109, 121
patents, 61, 106
PD, 117
penalties, 164
pension, 10, 18, 19, 52, 57, 66, 78, 90, 97, 103, 105, 106, 107, 109, 112, 120, 139, 140, 149
pension plans, 19, 90, 105, 107, 109, 112, 139
performance, 2
periodic, viii, 145
periodicity, 131
permit, 116, 140
personal, viii, 2, 9, 10, 12, 17, 18, 19, 26, 29, 30, 35, 38, 60, 64, 65, 66, 67, 68, 69, 71, 72, 75, 86, 87, 88, 90, 92, 93, 94, 98, 102, 103, 105, 107, 108, 109, 110, 111, 112, 113, 125, 127, 128, 135, 140, 142, 149, 157, 159, 160, 162
petroleum, 117
Petroleum, 138
planning, 2, 88, 90, 147
plants, 45, 154
play, 68
police, 71, 162
policymakers, vii, 2
population, 8, 25, 39, 93, 113
poverty, 4
power, 7, 88, 118
premiums, 54, 65, 106, 150, 152, 158, 159, 161
prescription drug, 164
price changes, 26, 117
price deflator, 29, 88, 117, 126, 127, 134
price index, 36, 89, 91, 114, 117, 127, 131, 132, 134, 136, 140
prices, 5, 9, 19, 26, 29, 37, 42, 88, 89, 102, 104, 106, 114, 115, 117, 118, 126, 131, 136, 138, 141
priorities, 91
private, 10, 11, 12, 13, 14, 15, 16, 17, 22, 23, 35, 38, 40, 57, 58, 59, 61, 66, 72, 73, 74, 76, 81, 84, 89, 90, 92, 94, 95, 98, 99, 100,

101, 102, 103, 104, 105, 106, 107, 108, 109, 111, 112, 113, 117, 120, 121, 122, 123, 124, 125, 128, 134, 135, 138, 139, 140, 147, 149, 154, 163
private enterprises, 12, 14, 16, 17, 57, 92, 103, 104, 105, 112, 139, 140
private investment, 35, 163
private sector, 89, 147, 149
proactive, 91
producers, 10, 12, 102, 118
production, viii, 2, 4, 5, 6, 7, 8, 9, 10, 11, 12, 13, 14, 15, 17, 18, 20, 27, 34, 35, 36, 37, 38, 39, 40, 45, 46, 48, 49, 50, 51, 52, 53, 55, 56, 57, 58, 59, 60, 61, 62, 63, 64, 65, 67, 69, 70, 73, 75, 76, 79, 84, 87, 89, 90, 92, 93, 94, 95, 98, 101, 102, 103, 106, 109, 111, 113, 118, 119, 138, 140, 142, 146, 147, 148, 154, 155, 156, 159, 160, 162, 164
productive capacity, 17, 43
productivity, 35, 89, 91
profit, 10, 57, 107, 118, 120, 122
profit margin, 118
profits, 2, 14, 16, 17, 22, 23, 41, 46, 49, 50, 51, 53, 54, 55, 57, 58, 59, 60, 61, 67, 74, 75, 77, 81, 85, 93, 94, 96, 100, 103, 105, 106, 107, 111, 123, 125, 138, 139, 157, 159
program, 162
promote, 155
property, 8, 10, 13, 19, 35, 46, 52, 53, 54, 62, 65, 67, 84, 89, 90, 93, 94, 102, 103, 109, 113, 135, 139
property taxes, 10, 52, 62, 67, 103
prostitution, 37
protection, 71
public, 11, 14, 20, 34, 37, 59, 69, 71, 89, 102, 110, 121, 143, 147, 158, 162
public debt, 20, 110
public education, 71
public goods, 11
public housing, 162
public policy, 34
Puerto Rico, 39, 83, 155
purchasing power, 7, 88, 118

R

radio, 154
real estate, 103, 106, 124
real property, 106
recessions, 129
recognition, 36
reconcile, 47
reconciliation, 128, 163, 164
recovery, 153
recreation, 124
Red Cross, 5
regional, 35, 91, 92
regression, 89
relationship, vii, 23, 34, 82, 86, 118, 157, 164
relationships, 86, 88
relative prices, 115, 116, 141, 142
reliability, 91, 129
Reliability, 28, 129, 143
remittances, 109, 135
rent, 10, 13, 62, 65, 107
repair, 119
resale, 89, 104
research, 54, 69, 90, 119
research and development, 119
researchers, 34, 88, 89
reserves, 109, 113
residential, 39, 101, 102, 103, 109, 135
residuals, 116
resources, 4, 6, 39, 41, 43, 53, 56, 57, 60, 61, 63, 70, 106, 124, 147, 155, 165
restaurant, 119
retail, 124
retained earnings, 17, 42, 45, 46, 148, 162
retirees, 149
retirement, 48, 66, 68, 72, 90, 107, 108, 109, 110, 140, 148, 149, 150, 151, 153, 163
returns, 45, 46, 59, 60, 74, 106, 121
revaluation, 138
revenue, 41, 43, 45, 49, 71, 104, 154
risk, 118, 140
rods, 139
royalties, 53, 61, 105, 106, 110, 158, 159
royalty, 46, 121
rural, 155

S

salaries, 11, 15, 18, 24, 49, 50, 52, 58, 64, 65, 70, 71, 76, 78, 95, 97, 101, 103, 107, 125, 143
salary, 15, 18, 21, 73, 76, 78, 80, 95, 97, 99, 103, 107, 110, 111, 125
sales, 6, 7, 13, 38, 45, 46, 48, 51, 52, 61, 63, 65, 67, 69, 71, 84, 93, 101, 102, 103, 112, 115, 118, 119, 120, 122, 123, 127, 138, 156
sample, 25
sample survey, 25
saving rate, 113
savings, 55, 68
scaling, 26
school, 155
seasonal pattern, 130
secondary education, 102
securities, 43, 44, 46, 47, 48, 109, 124
security, 11, 19, 66, 108, 109, 110
self-employed, 66
semiconductors, 137
Senate, 88
separation, 140
series, viii, 26, 31, 34, 45, 48, 104, 114, 115, 116, 121, 123, 124, 125, 127, 128, 129, 130, 134, 135, 139, 140, 141, 145
services, vii, 2, 3, 4, 5, 6, 7, 8, 10, 11, 13, 14, 15, 19, 21, 26, 35, 36, 37, 38, 39, 40, 41, 43, 44, 45, 46, 49, 50, 51, 52, 53, 54, 57, 58, 59, 61, 62, 63, 64, 65, 67, 69, 70, 71, 73, 75, 76, 80, 82, 84, 89, 90, 92, 93, 94, 95, 98, 99, 100, 102, 104, 105, 108, 110, 111, 112, 113, 114, 117, 118, 119, 120, 121, 123, 124, 129, 135, 138, 140, 142, 146, 147, 148, 155, 156, 158, 159
settlements, 66, 105, 108, 157
shareholders, 45, 47, 54, 75
shares, 29, 63, 116, 126
sharing, 107
short-term, 43, 44, 91
Short-term, 43, 44
short-term liabilities, 44
SIC, 122, 124
sign, 51, 138
sites, 143
smoothing, 157
social assistance, 108, 124
social benefits, 18, 19, 20, 66, 67, 69, 70, 78, 79, 97, 98, 108, 110, 161
social security, 11, 19, 66, 108, 110
Social Security, 153, 159, 161, 163
software, 4, 13, 14, 15, 36, 37, 39, 55, 76, 85, 90, 95, 101, 102, 111, 113, 120, 121, 122, 147
sole proprietor, 60, 61, 66, 106, 121
spectrum, 56, 154
speed, 89
SSI, 158
stages, 6
standards, 156
Standards, 137
statistics, 2, 8, 39, 88, 89
steel, 123
stock, 17, 39, 40, 44, 45, 47, 52, 83, 86, 88, 101, 103, 104, 107, 111, 122, 148, 159
strategic, 90, 91
Strategic Petroleum Reserve, 138
strategic planning, 90
streams, 42
structural changes, 37
students, 7, 83, 114
subsidies, 14, 20, 38, 52, 57, 62, 63, 65, 69, 94, 103, 139, 154, 159
subsidy, 147, 154
substitution, 115
summer, 125
supervision, 33, 145
supplemental, 29, 66, 108
Supplemental Security Income, 158
supplements, 52, 65, 103, 107, 111
suppliers, 93
surplus, 14, 15, 16, 17, 19, 20, 22, 38, 50, 51, 52, 53, 57, 58, 59, 61, 62, 64, 69, 70, 74, 76, 77, 79, 94, 95, 96, 98, 103, 104, 109, 110, 121, 122, 139, 148, 153, 155, 162, 163, 165
surprise, 40
survivors, 108
systems, 89, 91, 101, 120, 146

T

tangible, 35, 86, 100, 119
tax credit, 107
tax credits, 107
tax receipt, 20, 69, 70, 79, 98, 109, 159
taxation, 147
taxes, 10, 11, 14, 17, 18, 19, 20, 21, 22, 35, 38, 46, 47, 48, 51, 52, 54, 57, 60, 62, 63, 64, 65, 67, 69, 70, 75, 78, 79, 80, 94, 97, 98, 99, 102, 103, 107, 109, 111, 140, 143, 146, 147, 154, 157, 159, 161
tax-exempt, 60, 106, 121
telecommunications, 155
telecommunications services, 155
tenants, 102
textbooks, 84
theory, 14, 38, 93
time, vii, 2, 4, 8, 24, 25, 26, 30, 31, 34, 39, 42, 43, 44, 45, 62, 72, 83, 84, 88, 90, 91, 100, 114, 116, 119, 124, 125, 127, 129, 130, 141, 147, 156, 165
time increment, 147
time periods, 25, 127
time series, 26, 114, 130
timing, 20, 24, 148, 153, 157, 158, 163, 164, 165
title, 85, 91
tobacco, 106
total expenditures, 11, 14, 65, 71
total revenue, 163
tracking, 147
trade, vii, 2, 14, 22, 25, 118, 120, 124
trade deficit, vii, 2, 22
transactions, vii, 2, 3, 4, 5, 12, 14, 21, 22, 23, 24, 29, 34, 35, 37, 41, 42, 49, 53, 55, 56, 63, 65, 72, 74, 75, 76, 81, 83, 84, 85, 88, 92, 100, 101, 103, 112, 121, 122, 127, 128, 146, 147, 148, 149, 154, 155, 156, 157, 158, 163, 164
transfer, 11, 16, 17, 18, 19, 20, 21, 22, 23, 48, 49, 50, 52, 53, 54, 58, 64, 66, 67, 68, 69, 70, 71, 74, 75, 77, 78, 79, 80, 94, 96, 97, 98, 99, 102, 103, 105, 107, 108, 109, 110, 111, 147, 158, 159, 161, 163, 164, 165
transfer payments, 11, 16, 17, 18, 19, 20, 21, 22, 23, 48, 49, 50, 52, 53, 54, 58, 64, 67, 68, 69, 70, 71, 74, 75, 77, 78, 79, 80, 94, 96, 97, 98, 99, 102, 103, 105, 109, 110, 111, 158, 159, 161, 165
transportation, 119, 124, 154
travel, 119, 135
Treasury, 20, 146, 149, 164
Treasury Department, 20
trees, 36
trend, 129
trust, 94, 109, 149, 164
trust fund, 94, 109, 149, 164
trusts, 83, 85, 113, 124
tuition, 99

U

U.S. economy, vii, 2, 23, 34, 35, 90, 92, 117, 118, 146
U.S. military, 119, 138
unemployment, 20, 66, 108, 159, 161
unemployment insurance, 66, 108, 159, 161
United Nations, 82, 136, 164
United States, v, 2, 4, 8, 13, 16, 21, 22, 35, 39, 58, 60, 61, 68, 73, 74, 75, 76, 77, 80, 83, 84, 85, 87, 88, 89, 93, 94, 96, 99, 104, 105, 106, 107, 110, 111, 113, 114, 117, 118, 119, 128, 136, 137, 138, 139, 142, 146, 162
universities, 59

V

values, 5, 41, 62, 63, 74, 115, 117, 118, 129, 134, 135, 140
variance, 10
variation, 136
vehicles, 101, 124, 135
veterans, 108
voids, 137
volunteer work, 5

W

wage payments, 103
wages, 11, 15, 18, 24, 49, 50, 52, 58, 64, 65, 70, 71, 76, 78, 95, 97, 101, 103, 107, 125, 143
warehousing, 124
waste management, 124
water, 99, 154
wealth, 9, 19, 56, 68, 92
wear, 8, 40, 104
welfare, 94, 109
well-being, 4
wells, 101, 120, 141
wheat, 6
White House, 2
withdrawal, 5
witnesses, 139
workers, 11, 45, 62, 93, 120
workforce, 147
World Bank, 82, 136
World War, 27, 88
World War I, 27, 88
World War II, 27, 88